ME & MY MAMA'S

Tattoo

BY LYNNE D. SHIPLEY, MIT, ED.S.

PURPOSE PUBLISHING

Me and My Mama's Tattoo

Published with Purpose Publishing

Requests for permission to make copies of any part of the work should be sent to Lynne D. Shipley at www.edpop.net - Educating from a Position of Power! 816-866-8933

Me and My Mama's Tattoo edited by Melanie Greer
Book layout created and copyrighted by © 2016 by Lynne Shipley
Book cover art and design by Crimson Wings Graphics

Shipley, Lynne D.
    Me and My Mama's Tattoo/Lynne D. Shipley 1st Edition

ISBN: 9780997985344
Library of Congress Cataloging-in-Publication Data

Library of Congress Control Number: 2016960696
1.
2.
2. Title

Published by Michelle Gines, National Administrator PURPOSE PUBLISHING
www.PURPOSEPUBLISHING.com 816-401-7527 LIVE ~on~in~with~ PURPOSE

PURPOSE PUBLISHING

Printed in the United States of America

Me and My Mama's Tattoo

This book is dedicated to my parents.
Wayne and Diana Shipley.
Although they are no longer with me physically, they walk by my side daily. This project would have been in vain if I did not have my mom and dad to talk with during most of this journey. Their love, guidance and care when I became discouraged in the teaching profession, kept me moving forward.

Acknowledgements

Thank you to everyone who supported me during this seven year journey. When I initially discussed putting my students' conversations into a book, I received nothing but encouragement. Especially from my family.

I want to **shout out** to my extended family— the "lunch bunch", work colleagues, mentors, administrative supervisors and good friends. Your support has meant everything!

Finally, to my Lord and Savior, Jesus Christ, to Him be the glory.

Lynne D. Shipley

Table of Contents

Dear Reader,

This is my love letter. I hope it sparks uncomfortable dialogue. This love letter is addressed to educators who work with students from kindergarten to the high school. I wrote this book to talk about my desire to work with young people, and the issues I have encountered in educating them. I am not assigning blame for the decline of our educational system, nor am I providing a magical answer to make things better. This book is about conversations I've had with students and adults, whom I daily serve, and the avenues I have taken to be a better teacher. These stories represent true discussions on problems and issues I face daily as a teacher in an urban school.

"Me and My Mama's Tattoo" is written with the belief that in most homes the parents or guardians are the initial teachers and primary voice in their child' education. How the home views education, and how that view is conveyed to the child, shapes the learning philosophy of my students. As a teacher, I have no control over what happens in my students' homes. *I know this because my students tell me so.* If I make a request to a student that is contradictory to what they have learned at home, he or she will be vocal in letting me know they have been taught differently. Sometimes conflicting knowledge is based upon old wives tales, often it is based upon assumption and almost always it is a point of frustration and contention.

In my classroom, my role is to walk a fine line between teaching new and factual information while not impugning lessons from home. In other words, a teacher cannot say, "Your mama or daddy is wrong. Let me tell you how it really goes." Todays teachers have to be sensitive to their students' needs, while widening their window to the world. A teacher has to teach new concepts, use data to drive instruction, manage classroom behavior and expectations, competently teach a complicated curriculum to students with multiple learning styles — at times disabilities, while remaining poised, positive and productive, just in case an administrator or parent walks in for a surprise visit.

Teaching is not easy. As Ruby Payne, PhD states, "Teaching is a constant balancing act that requires firmness, insistence, high expectations, and support. It is certainly not a discipline for the faint of heart!"[1]

"Me and My Mama's Tattoo" offers seven stories that have impacted me while working in urban and high poverty schools. Teachers have stories to tell about their day to day interactions with students: this book presents stories that represent my experience and the experiences of my students. By highlighting specific conversations, I hope to make it easier for teachers to look behind a students' actions and behaviors and explore the root causes for their conduct. Many students walk into the school hungry, tired, economically challenged, abused and mistreated. Several come from loving and nurturing families and surroundings. The one thing the majority of my students have in common is their desire to be intelligent and to learn.

Regardless of their words, actions or deeds, no student wants to be treated as stupid or incapable of learning. A student might be inarticulate in their ability to address their wish to learn, but trust me it is in each and every one of them. Regardless of what it looks like on the outside; it is human nature to want to belong; and a school family is no different.

There is much outside interference from folks that are not educators. Todays schools are treated like businesses. Individuals, institutions and think tanks write policies on how to make our present school system better. There are "professionals" and "stakeholders" who believe they hold the keys to improving the urban educational process. I see people who do not live in the areas they teach. There are outside organizations that review school problems, plan studies, arrive at theoretical solutions and proceed to practice their experiments on inner city youth. I guarantee suburban parents would not let their children be pawns regarding their education. Parents, students, and teachers are caught in the crossfire. I see blame, plenty of money, but little progress or movement to increase student achievement in urban schools.

"Me and My Mama's Tattoo" uses comments students have made when there is no judgment or condemnation in their conversations. The declarations made by my students provided me with a view into their home lives and gives me insight into how they think and cope. I merged my conversations with facts, national trends and a few stats to provide a broader sense of understanding. It is time to stop asking "what can we do" and start doing. Even if that means starting all over again.

Today one can find anything on the internet, a cell phone or television. Radio plays music with lyrics that make old ladies blush. Videos provide images of naked bodies and acts that one has to be 18 or older to purchase. Because of unlimited access to adult content and themes, many children in the "urban core" come to school streetwise beyond their years. Teachers who do not reside in the same neighborhoods as their students do not understand the culture or climate where they work. It is important as a teacher to start listening nonjudgmentally to conversations students hold in the classroom, the hallway and on the playground in order to hear about the hidden lives of our kids. As a teacher, I advocate we stop befriending our students, and start respectfully teaching them by using humor, discipline and grace. It is imperative to prepare our students for the world they currently live in, and the one in which they need additional skills to succeed and excel. I recognize this is easier said than done, but I also know it can be done.

Each chapter begins with a vignette regarding a remark, act or conversation I've had in a class. Names have been changed, but the message remains consistent: our students and schools are in the fight of their lives. A few stories recount personal struggles, and some are sentiments "co-signed" by other students. One sentiment remains constant, students repeat what is modeled, not what they are told.

In addition to writing about my conversations, I hope to provide ideas that helped me when I found myself dumbfounded by a discussion or action that had taken place. I don't believe in stating problems without providing an answer that worked for me.

I have faith we can overcome tattoos of indifference with

education. The more factually based knowledge my students accumulate, the better they will be equipped to navigate the world. I hope to debunk stereotypes, and provide ammunition to start a discussion from the point of view of our children. Once we see with their eyes, and experience with their hearts, **we** can create an education system where our students shine.

I work in the trenches with parents who say they cannot make their students go to school or want to learn. Parents who have given up on 11, 12 and 13 year old children. My high school vice principal once asked, "How do you combat apathy?" In all of my reading, I have yet to see a study that addresses the issue of parental frustration. Where are the solutions to abject poverty, familial mental illness and generational anger, perpetual indifference. and the toll it takes on our children? Politics make light of these issues by blaming the community. Are we ready to take back our responsibility for teaching our young people? Clearly there are more questions than answers. So I write this book with a question asked by one of my principals, "how do you eat an elephant?" The answer, "One bite at a time." Consider this my taste.

Sincerely,

Lynne D. Shipley

Me and My Mama's Tattoo

Reflective Notes Pages

As instructors, we are asked to be reflective practitioners. After each chapter there are pages that allow the reader to write about an occurrence that resonates in their spirit.

$\diamond$

What is your story? – The space to write down a story that you have witnessed or been a party to that is similar. You can also write notes about the key issues in the chapter that you agree or disagree. Your story reflects just that…your story.

Websites and Articles – After writing your story, this is the place to list references and articles you have found that corroborate your story. You can list websites, magazines and publications, articles, seminars or anything else that will assist you in your quest for additional information.

Institutions, District or Local Resources – List the resources that will assist you in making a difference. This could include grant information, speaker bureaus, workshops, classes or anything that will help you or your student to be successful.

Action Plan – What are your plans once you have told your story? Using your research, information, and resources, create a plan to make a difference. This is the place to write your wonderful idea and start outlining the steps that will move your dreams and ideas to reality.

$\diamond$

**"Education is the most powerful weapon
which you can use to change the world."**

-Nelson Mandela

Chapter 1 –
Me and My Mama's Tattoo

The title "Me and My Mama's Tattoo" comes from a conversation I had one summer with an eleventh grade high school student I had known since he was in the seventh grade. A summer school teacher who was aware that I had taught David in middle school, asked me to address him falling asleep in class. She noted that he was failing and that if he did not pass summer school, he would not graduate on time.

The next time I saw him at lunch, I asked David what was going on in Mrs. Tompkins' class? He listened as I explained how important it was for him to turn in his assignments on time and not fall asleep in class. I offered to help him in any way I could, and asked if he needed a tutor. I knew David was working at the grocery store down the street from the school. I asked him if he thought he should cut back on some of his hours until he finished his summer course work.

Because I was his former teacher, David was always respectful. He thought about what I'd said for a moment and honestly replied, "Ms. Shipley, when I first started working I did not have a lot of hours. When I got my first paycheck, I barely had enough money for me and my mama's tattoo, so no I'm not going to cut back on my hours."

I said "Well, we all know what's important." We chatted

for a few more minutes, and I went back to my lunch duties.

I believe he left summer school that next week. I see David periodically around Kansas City. He never fails to say hello, and he is still a very nice young man. I do not know if David graduated from high school or has a G.E.D. I have never asked. But I do know his statement shaped how I viewed my students from that point forward.

I realized no matter what a teacher thinks of a students' home environment, all parents and guardians leave an indelible mark on their children. In his family, the value of getting a tattoo superseded his educational prospects. This viewpoint did not come from a television show or a song on the radio. Valuing a tattoo over his classes came directly from his mother.

Tattoos are "an indelible mark or figure fixed upon the body by insertion of pigment under the skin or by production of scars" as defined by the Merriam-Webster online dictionary.[2]

Getting a tattoo in itself is not a bad thing. I believe it should be a ritual reserved for adulthood. I realize more and more teenagers are permanently marking their bodies. If done correctly, the ink lasts a lifetime. My largest concern is that what we believe is "cool" in our youth can often bite us in the ass as we grow older. An improperly placed tattoo can lesson chances of landing certain jobs and provide small minded people with images that reinforce stereotypes.

During my conversation with David, I realized our families' brand (tattoo) us early on with opinions, facts, rituals and mores. Many beliefs last a lifetime and are passed from one generation to the next. These customs shape our opinions about what is important and what is not. His mother had inadvertently given him the impression that an external tattoo, an expensive picture of ink on the body, was possibly more important than getting a good education.

After my conversation with David, I started to pay attention to what my students said when they did not think an adult was listening. I began to eavesdrop about what they valued through their discussions with each other. I got the 411 on neighborhood gossip and which families were at war with each other. Students dropped the names of neighbors and fellow peers who were without utility services, and who was living with whom until "the heat got turned on". I heard how various kids were related, and who shared mothers and fathers. I found out who relied on government services, the date food stamps were received, and who would be "eating good" this weekend. Bullies were revealed, students were protected, and fights averted because of discussions held in the safety of Room 103 (my last classroom as a technology teacher).

When I first started teaching I honestly did not want to become involved with my students. I watched as teachers gave students their home phone numbers, social media monikers and invited kids to afterschool events or to their homes. I wondered how teachers could mix their personal and professional lives with the lives of their students. David changed my mind on everything.

I recognize that if I am to teach in the urban core, I cannot change my students' home circumstance, but I can do everything in my power to mitigate stereotypes that keep our students from achieving. In other words, the more I get in my students business, the better opportunity I have to offset adverse behaviors and provide them insight into a different world from the one they currently reside.

It is no secret amongst my peers, my administrators or my family that I believe as people of color we MUST live in two worlds in order to thrive. The earlier that lesson is understood, the better skills we develop to navigate our community. I am very clear with my students on how the world at large perceives urban culture and customs, and black people in particular. Although we own few media outlets, we have allowed our culture to be hijacked by news outlets. "Cultural appropriation" is the buzzword of today, but not everything is racist. We have to be honest about the negative stereotypes we perpetuate in our communities. Social media has multiplied the outlets we have available to promote Black pride and cultural successes. Yet I see negative images outnumber positive messages daily. Being Black in today's so-called "post-racial" society is no joke. It is confusing. It is challenging. It is rife with perplexing images.

Valuing a tattoo over passing a class is a prime example of choosing what our family values over the advancement of oneself through the educational process. Devaluing education elicits dire repercussions. Although the dropout rate has decreased, it continues to be a disproportionally high number for Blacks and Hispanics. According to the article "National High School Graduation Rates Improve" by Jason Koebler a report in *Education Week* stated "about 72 percent of public school students from the class of 2008 graduated on time, a 6 percentage-point increase from the 1997 rate".[3] That same article goes on to state the "rates for Blacks and Hispanics is 57 percent."

The Schott Report is gender specific. It states in "2012-13 the estimated graduation rate for Black males was 59%." For Latino males, the rate was approximately 65 percent"[4]. Although an increase over previous years, what this says to me is that a little under 3 in 5 Black males graduated high school on time; and Latino males did slightly better.

At what point does a parent approve of their child not attending school? When confronting parents about their students' undesirable behavior, a mother or father often argues the behavior the teacher describes in school is opposite to the way their child acts at home. Many times I disagree. As a teacher, I constantly overhear conversations between students and their parents. Students who use unsuitable language when talking to a teacher, often use inappropriate language towards their family during a parental meeting.

Respect for education starts at home. Just as respect for the principal, the teacher, other school officials and members of the community, start at home. Parents who display the value of education with their students at an early age create students who are eager to learn and also value education. As parents start to take responsibility for the actions of their children in the classroom and start holding their students accountable for learning, passing classes, attendance and grades, we can turn our attention to other issues affecting gains in student achievement.

Cell Phones versus Sell Phone

Education and the act of learning are to be admired, encouraged, and exemplified. It should not come at the expense of a tattoo. Learning is an act of courage. Scholarship is the legacy of my forefathers and foremothers, and it is the TRUE inheritance of the community from which I come, and of which I serve. No parent wants their child to become the neighborhood thief, drug addict or 'ho (whore). All parents want better for their children than themselves. Yet this sentiment is not fully articulated in word or deed.

It is true we live in a different world than our grandparents. First and foremost, there is the internet. Secondly, the cell phone. The world-wide-web has changed the way we communicate with each other and has moved the universe into our living rooms. Communicating through social networking is the norm. According to the Pew Research Center "Approximately, 79%[5] of online adults use Facebook. Young adults are the most likely to say they use social media sites, while <u>men have recently caught up with women</u> in overall social media use. *Urban dwellers are more likely than rural users to be on social media. Women, African-Americans, and Latinos show high interest in sites like Twitter, Instagram and Pinterest.*" (I put in the bold italics.)

In 2012, the Pew Research Center's Internet & American Life Project survey broke down a graph labeled "The Landscape of Social

Media Users". There were five networking sites listed on the chart, Facebook, Twitter, Pinterest, Instagram and Tumblr. Of these five, the two social networks most appealing to 18-29 year old African Americans and urban residents were Twitter and Tumblr. It is my view that with a third party account, a person can tweet anonymously with a 140 word limit. This allows one to post secretly and fire off rapid rants and quick responses to many followers at one time. Tumblr has more flexibility for its posts. Approximately 10% of all social network users use Tumblr, but its popularity is rapidly growing.

Cell phones provide instantaneous communication to anyone in the world, via text, talk or email. New smartphones are hand held computers that hold more power "than NASA in 1969".[6] "There are video games and many more technological wonders that did not exist 30 years ago. So, when immature minds are provided unfettered access to adult videos, pictures, music and language at the click of a button, without being provided mature guidance on how to separate fact from fiction — they suffer immensely. I have observed my student's behavior for the last nine years, and for the first time in my teaching career, I am adamant that as educators we must do something radically different or the school system in place will fail our young people. If we continue along the current path, our society will pay a large price for the future.

I advocate providing students with flip phones. If they want to use social media, then their parents can get a tablet or a computer. But only flip phones should be allowed in the class, especially as we move to 1 to 1 technology. If students are provided tablets, then the cell phones become redundant. A flip phone will provide them the basic telephone in a pocket or purse, and provide instant communication.

The students I teach are inundated with what looks like unearned materialistic trappings of success. My students constantly have the latest in technology and shoes. In our discussions, they express three legal ways to get rich. They can be entertainers (rapper, singer, actor), a sports figure (primarily football or basketball), or they can do well in school and hope to go to college, the military or trade school. The predominate profession when I ask my young ladies is often lawyer or doctor. Young men select athlete.

One of my teaching friends rushed down to show me a students' paper who wrote down his chosen profession. To the question "what are your plans when you grow up?" He wrote "I want to play football or be a raper." I am quite sure he meant rapper, and equally positive he had no idea what he wrote.

Every student expresses plans to go to college, but in middle school these kids have grade point averages below 2.0. For boys, going to college often ranks a distant third. Many of my young men think they are going to "make it" playing basketball or rapping. Of course "slinging" (selling drugs) is always an option, but few students candidly talk about it. Although I did have a young man (again a former middle school student) allude to it one day. I told him I would prefer he didn't choose that line of "work". He told me that he wouldn't refer to it again around me. I didn't shut him down, and he knew I did not approve, yet in making that statement he wanted to see if I would negatively react.

Students are given regular doses of mixed messages. In order to be successful, a person must look like this, have this type of job, drive this kind of car and live in a big house. What ever happened to all honest work is good work? In this new information age, it is important for parents to be knowledgeable of social media and open to different types of conversations. Especially in our urban homes, so students don't get left behind. There must be a dramatic shift how we impart information to our kids. Young people "do what they see", not what we tell them to do. If we want our children to have a better life, as adults we must be willing to create a better life for ourselves.

The website Blackdemographics.com examines the labor force participation rates according to race. The number of Blacks employed in

2000 was 65%. That number dropped to 64% in 2010. Consequently, the number of Hispanics working remained the same at 68%. Hispanics were the highest group for labor force participation. Whites went from 67% to 66% from 2000 to 2010 and Asians remained the same at 67%. [7]

So if 64% of all African Americans are employed, in what industry does this population work? According to a chart on Blackdemograhics.com that categorizes the African American workforce by industry as reported by the 2011 US Census Bureau A.C.S., "29.5% of all African Americans in the workforce are in government jobs such as education, social assistance, and public administration."[8] The next industry is retail (11.2%) followed by arts, entertainment, and recreation (9.6%). Roughly 50% of the African American population workforce is concentrated in three industrial segments out of the thirteen that are listed. That means that the remaining ten employable areas of trade share 50% of Black workers. For me, this represents opportunity lost. By minimizing the value of education, we limit our children's prospects.

We must be vigilant in what we let our young people see. When they see that education and working is not important in their homes, it becomes unimportant to them. When students tell me the financial inner workings of where they live, I know they have been privy to adult conversations. I do not believe that children and young adults should be aware of all of the information that stems from the adults in a household. A child and parent cannot co-parent each other together. The parent must lead by example. That means monitoring internet behavior, setting boundaries, being aware of what is said in front of the children, participating in their schooling and limiting negative exposure while increasing new and positive experiences. In other words, parent.

We have got to give our babies the message that there is no shame in being smart. There is no shame in wanting to be valedictorian, striving for straight "A's" or graduating from high school with a grade point average of 2.0 or better. There is no shame in dreaming and failing, or of being wrong and trying again. There is no disgrace in desiring a better life, of speaking properly, of writing wonderfully and of pursuing a vision that is foreign to the world in which we were born. In fact, isn't that the way the United States became a great nation, by overcoming the impossible, envisioning a different future and pursuing a better life for our future generations?

The last time I saw David I barely recognized him. The boy I taught in middle school is now a man. He is taller, with a full mustache and beard. When he saw me he asked "Ms. Shipley, do you remember me?" I smiled, nodded and gave him a hug. We talked briefly and I continued into the store. I am pleased to know he has a regular job, an honest job. I hope he is living the life he imagined for himself. He does have one addition and that is a neck tattoo.

Reflection Notes

What is your story?

_____

_____

_____

_____

_____

_____

_____

_____

_____

_____

_____

_____

_____

_____

_____

_____

_____

_____

_____

_____

Reflection Notes

Websites and Articles:

1. _____

2. _____

3. _____

4. _____

5. _____

6. _____

7. _____

Institution, District or Local Resources:

1. _____

2. _____

3. _____

4. _____

5. _____

6. _____

7. _____

Reflection Notes

Action Plan: _____

Date: _____

_____

_____

_____

_____

_____

_____

_____

_____

_____

_____

_____

_____

_____

_____

_____

_____

_____

_____

Me and My Mama's Tattoo

Chapter 2 –

Ugh! You Teach Middle School. I'm Going to Pray for You!

In 2013, I had a student who kept sleeping in In School Suspension (ISS). I asked him why he was so tired. He informed me that his mother had called him from somewhere, and wanted him to stay awake to open the door for her when she arrived home. I asked what time she came in and he replied, "She didn't." This baby stayed up all night waiting for his mother. A mother who did not have the decency to notify her child she would not be coming in that evening, and instead of waiting up for her, to go to bed. I told him to go ahead and sleep. Pray for young folks like him, not me.

After I got my Master's in Information Technology I decided to teach middle school. I had something to offer the youth of today, and by God I was going to save our community by becoming a teacher. I contacted a relative who worked in an urban school district, applied, interviewed and was put to work. I researched and was accepted into the Missouri Transition to Teaching Program. The Transition to Teaching Program was federal program designed to assist mid-career professionals who wanted to take an alternative route into the field of education. In the fall of 2004, I entered Martin Luther King, Jr. Middle School as the new computer teacher and was immediately smacked in the face with reality.

Before I go further, let me tell you about my familial tattoo. My mother, Diana Gail Bradley Shipley, was a principal by the time she retired from education. Wayne Douglas Shipley, my father, was a financial analyst. Until I was 13, I would help my mom put her classroom together every August. I grew up grading papers. I watched her work hard and eavesdropped on her conversations as she discussed her students with fellow teachers and friends. When I was around 10, mom earned her Master's Degree in Psychology. I watched her study, and eventually my brother and I became her favorite test subjects. While our friends played kickball and hide and seek outside, we were being subjected to the Rorschach test, flash cards and any other form of psychological testing my mother deemed necessary to complete her degree. I knew early on I had a Type A personality. I tried to use this knowledge to my advantage like; "if you remember Mom, I have a Type A personality, so when the teacher said this…I just had to say that…" Of course, it never made a difference, but as a teenager, it was worth a try.

My mother was a teacher and counselor. She was a race relations facilitator, World Book salesperson, vice principal, award winning principal and consultant. As an unwavering advocate of the Comer School Development Program she attended more than a few classes at Yale, and became a published author and speaker around Southern California. My mom and dad were my greatest role models and the epitome of success; both valued education. But this "mom lady" was popular, beautiful, smart and well-known in our community. Still, I solemnly vowed NEVER to become an educator. They worked too hard and were paid too little.

Soon after I began my new career, my mother announced she was coming for a visit. I later learned she wanted to see my classroom and watch me teach. I foolishly thought she was coming for a friendly visit. It was not until **after** she came that I realized she flew 1,200 miles to give me my first evaluation.

Mom sat in the back of my class for two days. She said very little and took no notes. She would nod her head when a lesson was going particularly well, and shake her head when I let the class get out of control. I was a new teacher and had no idea what I was doing. On the eve of her second day she said, "I came here prepared to tell you to get out of teaching. I couldn't imagine you as a **good** teacher, and we have enough **bad** teachers as it is. I think you will do fine. You need some coaching, but you like the kids and that's the first step." Relieved, I received my mother's blessing to become a teacher.

Of course, I was floored. What I thought was a visit to support me in my new endeavor was actually a test. I often tell this story to new teachers because, as my mother stated, bad teachers need to be weeded out of the profession early on. There are usually one of two reactions to my story: people can't believe that my mother would be so hard on me, or they laugh and instantly understand why I am the way I am.

To have known Diana was to know honesty in the flesh. My mother knew I had received a B.S. in Marketing, and a Master's in Information Technology. I had worked in radio sales and printing. Why in the hell did I want to teach? In order for her to be at peace with MY decision, it became her mission to find out whether or not I would damage children in the profession she loved. If I was not a good teacher, she would have told me. And I would have found something else to do.

Middle School for Me

There are several selfish reasons why I chose the mid-grade level. First, they are no longer small people who need a lot of assistance. Elementary school students, as cute as they are, need a lot of attention. I am not that patient or kind. I stand up and applaud elementary school teachers because they are generally easygoing, collaborative and work tirelessly to ensure their children succeed. K – 5 teachers are tear dryers, doctors, psychologists and applauders.

I did not select high school because this age generally thinks they are grown. I don't do well with 15 – 18 year olds who don't know much, have no jobs, pay no taxes but want to speak to you as if they are adults. High school teachers are also special. They enjoy ushering our older teenagers into adulthood, discussing large themed subjects and in general teaching critical skills our students will need to move into the future.

I chose to teach 11 – 14 year-olds at age 40. Middle school teachers are in a class of their own. They contend with students as they transform from babyish children to teenagers. We work with kids who have raging hormones, insecurities, narcissistic attitudes and who are in a constant state of flux. Their parents are often confused, and the students are confused too. In order to teach middle school, one must have a knack for working with smart ass kids. I do. I am a smartass adult. It is my goal to leave my students smarter than when they entered my classroom. I tell my students this every semester. My goal is to provide them with a safe classroom where they are free to make mistakes, free to challenge themselves and free to learn. It was important for me to find my fit as a teacher. I teach a subject I love, to an age group I am fond of, and I flourish as a person. It is a perfect fit.

So it pisses me off when a person I have never met before asks me what I do for a living and after saying, "I teach middle school technology" they reply with, "Ugh! You teach middle school? I wouldn't want your job, or I'm going to pray for you, there must be a special place for you in heaven!" In my mind I think, "WTF? These are *your* children, if you think my job is so terrible because I work with your kids, what does that say about you as a parent?"

The Profession of Teaching

According to the 2010 census[9], there are 7.2 million teachers in the United States. There are almost 3 million elementary school teachers, which leaves over 4 million who teach secondary school, pre-k, post-secondary, special education and other types of instruction. The average salary nationally in 2010 was $52,800. California teachers averaged the highest wage at $65,800 in 2006-07, and teachers in South Dakota averaged the lowest rate of pay at $36,700. A friend of mine likened teaching to being the most "educationally accomplished blue collar profession in the country". I concur.

In September, 2012, CNN was one of the countless news outlets that produced a teacher segment on why teachers remain in the profession. NBC produces a program called "Education Nation" which highlights the nation's school system. There have been articles written by journalists from the New York Times to the Sacramento Bee about teachers, parents, students and the process of instructing our youth. There are parent initiatives, hundreds of university programs, thousands of websites; immeasurable hours spent interviewing "specialists" and countless consultants telling us what is wrong with the state of education and how to fix it. Blame is rampant and attributed to everyone, from the teacher, student, parent, neighborhood, and economy to the "system" at large.

With all of this hoopla, it is a wonder any college or university student majors in education. The field has been demonized and vilified as being the most broken part of the educational process. Let's be honest, the pay is terrible. Professional athletes and business executives make millions, while the teachers make pennies on the dollar. From what I can tell, the new breed of superintendents spouts the mantra that teachers are the main problem and, everything else is…great.

It takes a teacher to tell the world that educators are the glue that holds the task of schooling our youth together.

That is the message that the Chicago Teachers Union got across to the public when they went on strike in September 2012. The Chicago strike only affected Chicago; but it was watched closely by teachers, administrators and school boards throughout the country. The concessions made on both sides create a blue print for future negotiations regarding teacher pay and teacher responsibility. Unfortunately, that glue did not hold for long, and many things the teachers fought for were unraveled in the following years.

Most teachers teach because they enjoy being a part of a child's successful entry into the world. That is one of the major reasons I teach. I enjoy opening up new avenues for my students to explore. I encourage them to seek answers and truths for themselves. I marvel at their curiosity, and hopefully create a safe space where they believe it is right to sometimes be wrong.

The one secret most urban teachers share is that regardless of the desire, we know we are incapable of reaching every student. We do well if we reach one or two per year. Now that I have let the genie out of the bottle, let's go one step further. The grand idea that one teacher, can create 30 unique learning style profiles, use differentiated instruction and successfully fulfill every child's wants and needs, in a classroom where students range from Gifted and Talented to special needs is *ludicrous*.

In the past, classroom norms were established by the teacher. Teachers lectured, allowed students to work in small groups or pairs, required students to create projects, write papers and make whole group presentations. Ideally, parents assisted the teacher in working with their child as they moved from grade to grade. The way I learned was through skill and drill, lecture, competition (remember the blue bird and red bird reading groups) and recitation. My elementary teachers were thoroughly engaged in my daily lessons. As I became older, most of my teachers stuck to the lecture format, or the occasional project. Even though I attended two laboratory schools growing up, the majority of my experiences mimicked my parents. To augment my learning, my folks filled our home with flash cards, books, field trips, documentaries and other learning tools that would enlarge our perspective.

In today's schools, teachers turn in lesson plans at the beginning of each week. Each plan has to be engaging, conform to state standards, be in line with the district curriculum and have specific learning targets. The lesson must also be rigorous, appealing and informative. Administrators look for teachers who proactively use technology, practice differentiated instruction and in general are a "jack of all educational and curriculum trades". Not only is this expected in their daily classroom instruction, teachers are expected to quiz weekly and use their collaborative data to drive instruction. Whoa! I get tired just thinking about it. Does it sound like I'm bitching? I am not. I am just trying to paint the picture with what we educators deal with daily.

With budget cuts in school funding, lower tax revenues, reductions in paraprofessionals and other staff, and the elimination of programs that assist our students in succeeding, we are constantly asked to do more with less. When talking to lay people, I often hear "teachers have it really good, you know with summers off and stuff". Or I am asked, "Why aren't your students achieving on the same level as their suburban counterparts?" It is true that every child deserves a positive classroom experience, but it is unreasonable to place the onus solely upon the backs of teachers as the main group responsible for educating today's student. Especially in the contentious society we live in today.

Remember the book, <u>It Takes a Village</u> by Hillary Rodham Clinton. This book was an insight to what we as a society can do to make this a better world for our children. For a brief moment, we as a nation really looked upon our children as the key to our future, our passport into the next millennium. Although teachers are an important part of our children's lives, it is the parent or parental figure that sets the tone on how he or she will compete in society. It is the parent who instills the love of learning in their children.

In the last 25 years (zero tolerance policies), I fear the profession of teaching has gone from an art and science to a magic show. Especially in urban settings. We are expected to miraculously take students who are below grade level - often over aged, and get them caught up to their appropriate grade level in reading and math. Now this is not impossible. We have seen movies and television shows where a teacher comes in and creates a wonderful classroom environment where all of the students change their errant ways and become fruitful. There are YouTube videos and books written by teachers that have made great strides in urban education. Sadly, these stories are few and far between. In truth, students fall somewhere in between. Many of my students catch up and move forward, but there are still a few that fall through the cracks. Unfortunately, there are also some who enter the juvenile justice system and never come back.

Honesty Can Drive Policy

We can increase student achievement when the educational system is honest about the population of students they serve. Every district and board should be required to take a demographic assessment of the poverty rate, employment and housing statistics in their community. We must stop believing there is a "one size fits all" approach that will cure all ills. Each district should be required to take a hard look at their city, and address the issues that impede educational parity.

School districts are responsible for employing and training teachers who can teach and relate to the people of that community. If a district wants to know how to improve the educational process, maybe they should listen to the teachers and administrators who work with this group daily. It is important to select all types of teachers, not just the star teacher who everyone believes is doing a yeoman's job. Enlist the struggling teacher, the new teacher, the teacher who is about to retire; it is this segment of the profession that will provide an honest and unbiased view of the day to day dealings in a classroom. If I am a struggling teacher, I am going to tell you where I believe the system has failed. If I am a new teacher, I will let you know where I could use more help: If I am a retiring or long term teacher, I might have a handle on what worked in the past.

My hope is that district offices across the country stop listening to every "Tom, Dick and Harry" who comes along with a new study about how to raise test scores in the urban community, and start to listen to the professionals they have hired and trained. Quit hiring outside consultants and paying them hideous amounts of money to tell school boards and superintendents the same things teachers have been discussing for years. It does not take an expert to corroborate truth.

The Economics of Teaching

A lot of my fellow teachers have part-time jobs, including myself, so we can make ends meet. To hear politicians and political analysts discuss how ineffective we are, is a knife to the gut. They talk about how much money we make, coupled with having summers off, obviously teaching must be a cushy job, and anyone can do it.

Of course, there are some terrible teachers; there have always been a small group of bad teachers. Look at the social and structural changes our educational system has gone through in the last two hundred years. To think that all teachers view the profession as a calling is crazy. Teaching employs its share of unprofessional people like any other career. There are many mechanisms to root out teachers who exhibit immoral acts. There are fewer options available to get rid of ineffective teachers.

When this country was founded it was illegal for a black woman born into slavery, to learn to read and write. I teach in the city in which I was born, Kansas City, Missouri. Missouri has addressed African Americans in the public schools since 1867 in response to the constitutional changes in 1865. In 1921, the Department of Education in Missouri established an Inspector of Negro Schools. The last official to serve in this office was my cousin Alonzo Redmon. After the Brown vs. Board of Education decision in 1954, this office was kept until 1958[10.]

According to the web page module, "What Happened to All the Black Principals after Brown?"[11] by Maurice Smith and Linda Lemasters, the educational system for African Americans underwent significant changes for the first 10 years after the landmark Brown decision. It is my belief that students who had teachers that looked like them, and that came from their communities, were no longer welcome in the newly designed desegregated system. Students were required to integrate, but the profession of teaching was not.

My parents entered high school in a legally integrated system. Both entered the 9th grade in the 1955 school year. Both were members of an integrated class that matriculated in 1959, and both graduated from Lincoln University, a Historically Black College/University.

They both talked fondly about going to school with children of the same race. Although they did not have new books, and used sports equipment, they knew they were loved by their teachers and considered smart. Even thought my mother enjoyed her high school years at an integrated school in a small town, my father does not speak kindly about his high school experience. He talks about how prejudiced many of his teachers were, how difficult it was to be a smart black man in a historically white school, and the institutionalized racism he had to overcome daily. He no longer saw the Black teachers who had mentored him as a boy. His teachers became obstacles that he had to overcome.

My brother and I were part of the bussing generation, and although schools were no longer legally segregated, I can count the Black teachers I had on one hand. We had educated parents who gave us many experiences that education cannot buy. We ate dinner together almost nightly, were versed in the art of conversation, played sports and were considered "good kids". Both of us went to college, and both of us have "good jobs". I say all of this because I was raised to be successful. The definition of success in my house was to work at a job that makes you happy, find hobbies you enjoy, communicate with your family (and those you call family) and have fun in life. My father often says if you have these things, then you are successful. He never mentioned money, or fame, but he was big on love and happiness.

So, if teachers are not in it for the money, why do we teach? I teach because all children deserve a good education regardless of race. I teach because it makes me happy. I teach because it is the way I serve my community. It is my calling to provide a good educational foundation for the populace I engage. Whether it is in a desegregated environment, or a newly re-segregated school, all students in America have a RIGHT to a good education. I teach because I want to be a part of a grassroots movement that makes this constitutional right a reality!

In 2014, the number of whites students that attended public schools fell below 50% for the first time.[12] Yet, 43% of Latino children and 38% of African American children attend school where less than 10% of the student body is white.[13] This means those children do not intersect with the majority population. In these same schools, the majority of teachers are white. According to the 2011 Center for Progress report "Increasing Teacher Diversity Strategies to Improve the Teacher Workforce" only 14% of all teachers are Black or Latino. This means many of my students are taught by people that do not look like them. I can attest to the fact that in the 2009-2010 school years, I don't believe one of my co-workers had students that attended school in our district. Teachers who live in the suburbs, and have no connection to the student's they teach, are responsible for schooling a group of children they do not understand. The above statement is not meant to be judgmental, for me it is a fact.

Although I try not to attach any type of judgment to suburbanites teaching urban kids, the truth is, I do judge. Teachers were a vibrant part of the minority community when I grew up. It was one of the few professions where Blacks were "allowed" to thrive. My sixth grade teacher, Mrs. Johnson, lived two blocks from our house and the school. It was not strange to bicycle past her house and see her outside watering her flowers. This was typical of the times. Now, I watch as many of my co-workers race the busses to get the "hell out of dodge", and back to the safety of their communities. By the way, this also includes teachers of color.

Today is a new day, a new time, and many professions that were closed are now open to people of all genders and races. I sound critical because I have a lot of feelings regarding our educational system and how they teach Blacks, Latinos and Asians. Many of my students are kinesthetic, and learn more actively than when I did as a child. If we have teachers who are disconnected from their students, how can they be expected to teach students they don't understand? I do not advocate urban teachers living in urban neighborhoods. Nor do I believe that you have to be a person of color (POC) in order to teach students of color. I do believe that race relations and human relations must be a part of a district's professional development strategies if we are to teach a diverse student population. To accept that this elephant in the room does not exist means that an integral part of moving students forward is ignored.

Growing up, I attended six elementary schools. Not because I was a behavior issue, but because my parents moved in search of better opportunities for themselves; therefore, better opportunities for my brother and I. In school, I had many positive experiences and my fair share of negative ones as well. I don't believe that there is a direct correlation between the race of the teacher and the success of students of a different color. It is true, good teachers come in every race, gender, religion and sexual orientation. There is one fact that can't be denied, the influx of more minorities in public schools over the last 50 years, coupled with the decrease in teachers of color during this same time period, has seen student achievement among urban educated youth fall to an all-time low.

When I tell people I am a teacher, I say it proudly, regardless of their crass remarks. The negative reaction to my career is disconcerting. As an African American teacher, I refuse to believe our children are less than, are incapable of, or don't know how to learn — as has been stated in at least three lunch rooms where I have taught. I believe all scholars deserve the best education available at every level that leads to achievement and accomplishment. Therefore, I teach the children of people who are praying for me (and for all of us who teach) because dammit, I am the right person to teach the students of today. I teach because regardless of what the media, political pundits and my salary say, teaching is a noble profession. I teach because children need people who believe in them, even when many members of our society say they are ignorant, dumb or stupid. I teach because although this is my third career, it is the career I was born to do. I teach because someone I don't know prayed I would.

For all of you who think teaching is the worst job on earth, I earnestly say this to you…we teach *your* children. So, if you are fearful for me, remember you are responsible for the creation you send me daily. After all is said and done, I take the child you are praying for me about, and teach him or her how to read, execute mathematical problems, learn about history, perform experiments, and create technological wonders that boggle the mind. Every adult in this country is a product of a teacher.

Instead of praying for us, spend time with your child and assist them in becoming ready for school. Ensure they get the proper nutrition and enough sleep. Welcome their enthusiasm about their daily lessons in conversation. Help them with their homework. Volunteer at the school, go on field trips and be present for parent teacher conferences. Be honest about who your child is, taking assistance when it is offered and encourage them to be smart. READ to them. There is a simple saying that goes, "If you want to keep knowledge from minority students, put it in a book." Parents, instead of video games, buy books. Read to your children early and often. Buy or build your child a book case and find them a place to study. These small gestures tell your student that education is important and has a place of value in your home.

I believe apathy can be addressed with fact-based information, authentic conversation, an honest picture of the current state of our schools, a set of goals to be achieved, and a staff willing to collaborate amongst themselves, the students, parents and the community. Then together, a plan should be created: a malleable plan which can be modified regularly. With a sufficient plan in place, a school can press forward in obtaining their goals. Each school is different and faces a unique set of challenges. A district that does not address the individuality of each learning institution, and formulates one set of rules across the district is doomed for failure. There is a sports analogy which states, "To rise, one must fall."[14] In order to teach, one must fall, and fall often; but falling is not failure. Each time a teacher stands, each day he or she returns to their classroom, it presents another opportunity to reach one more student.

I would appreciate no more negative comments about my profession when I tell you I teach for a living. My answer to all those naysayers is, "All teachers teach to make a difference; be it positive or negative." If we partner together, students and teachers, parents and administrators; school districts and their communities, I know we can make a difference. Across racial lines, gender roles and any other differences that makes this country great.

Reflection Notes

What is your story?

_____

_____

_____

_____

_____

_____

_____

_____

_____

_____

_____

_____

_____

_____

_____

_____

_____

_____

_____

Reflection Notes

Websites and Articles:

1. _____

2. _____

3. _____

4. _____

5. _____

6. _____

7. _____

Institution, District or Local Resources:

1. _____

2. _____

3. _____

4. _____

5. _____

6. _____

7. _____

Reflection Notes

Action Plan: _____

Date: _____

_____

_____

_____

_____

_____

_____

_____

_____

_____

_____

_____

_____

_____

_____

_____

_____

_____

_____

Me and My Mama's Tattoo

Chapter 3 -

TNT – Too Nice Theory

One Friday afternoon, I leave my students with another teacher because I am scheduled to grade my senior student's presentation. I turn on a movie we started the day before, the teacher comes in on schedule and I leave with my usual words of wisdom, "Please give this teacher the same respect you give to me."

Thirty minutes later, I come down the hall and heard loud talking from my class as I approached the room. As I got closer to the closed door, I notice the movie is playing, yet students are out of their seats, several students are now sitting close to the teacher and the movie is playing to an inattentive audience. I look at the teacher, who sees the irritated look on my face and blurts out, "I told ya'll to be quiet". I thank him and send him on his way.

I sit down, turn the movie off right before it climaxes, and face to class. After all of the students are in their assigned seats, I ask them, "What is the problem?" I go on to explain that I cannot believe that they would disrespect this teacher in my class. I tell the class whenever I enter "Mr. Smith's" room they are in disarray. Students are up playing and talking over him as he tries to teach, in general being disruptive. I ask in a very stern voice, "What is wrong with you all? Why do you treat my colleague the way you do?" Then one of my most quiet students says, "He's too nice." I shake my head and I say to myself..."wow."

There is an adage that says if you want to be an effective teacher, and gain classroom control from the first day of a new school year, you don't smile until after Christmas. Now I am not sure if that is true or not, but most students can smell a new teacher a mile away. Teachers who enter the profession, as my mother used to say, "wide eyed and bushy tailed" are often blind-sided by savvy students who view "too nice" teachers as easy bait.

To be fair, I was a new teacher who wanted to be liked by my students. I thought that since I had worked in the private sector, I had a lot to offer this group of kids that a seasoned, professional teacher might have missed. Boy was I wrong.

I stated earlier my mother came to visit me shortly after I started teaching. Although the "Chief" gave me her blessing, I still had a lot to learn. I had to learn to walk a line between classroom manager, instructor and empathizer, while fostering creativity and solidarity among my students. In most districts, the ultimate test of being an effective teacher are test scores. Although this one measurement is simplistic, it is the metric which all teachers, schools and districts are measured. It is not stated publicly, but a teacher who moves student's academically is prized over a teacher who does not. Even a seasoned teacher is expected to adhere to these expectations. The one true statement I can make is that I felt lost.

The first school I was assigned to was coming off a disastrous school year and they were designated as a "turn around school". The school was given a new principal, teachers were moved there from another closed middle school. Administrators were tasked with improving test scores, decreasing suspension rates and uplifting morale, in one of the most economically and crime ridden zip codes in Kansas City, MO.

The school was built with an open concept in mind, and NO windows. Because there was an opening above each classroom door, students would throw things into the classes, including lit matches and fire crackers. Fights were prevalent, students test scores were low, and the staff complained constantly in the break room. It was disheartening to say the least.

I was blessed as a new teacher to have four seasoned professionals assist me in learning the business of teaching. If I had not met these four women during my first few years, I am not sure if I would have had the strength to continue. These teachers, and my first administrative team, assisted me professionally, personally and academically when I began my coursework for my Education Specialist degree, academically. My colleagues made themselves accessible to me at all times, and there was no question too small or inane. They encouraged me when I was down, pulled me back from the brink when I was angry or upset at the system, and supported me on various projects that I embarked upon for the sake of my students.

My cohorts were honest with me about my negative actions when things were not going my way, and helped me soar professionally. There was nothing I could not share, nothing I could not ask and nothing that kept me from growing as a person and educator.

It also helped that I was willing to listen. Listening to co-workers who are more accomplished and mature in teaching helped me tremendously. It was my team leader who told me that she was going to groom me in my third year of teaching to take over her position. It was my instructional coach who explained to me that after two years my classroom walls could no longer be bare and had to reflect student work. It was the drama teacher down the hall that year after year demonstrated though her students' work how creative and smart our "bad" kids were. I had role models all around me, and although I was 41 when I started teaching, I was not too young to learn, and learning meant taking notes, failing and trying again.

In our culture, it is not popular to admit our shortcomings and possible failures. Fortunately, I was not raised (tattooed) to think asking for help was wrong. In fact, it was encouraged in my house to ask for assistance. No one was going to do all of the work, but they would point me in the right direction and not yell at me if I made a mistake. This was HUGE! I grew up with a sense of security that if I failed, I could pick myself up and try again. For many of us, we are made to feel like a failure if we are not number one, or if we make an error. Even though I was ok with asking questions, and not always being successful the first time around, this was the complete opposite in the field of education. I felt when one admits to failing in the educational field, it is tantamount to failing children. I was fortunate to be given a learning curve, not every teacher is as lucky.

In my opinion, I feel many educators of today are products of pre -packaged education courses. Goods of outdated teacher programs designed with a set of theoretical instructions to make any and every one who wants to teach successful. There are programs where teachers go to a few classes during the summer after they graduate from college, and teach in an urban classroom in the fall. To place new teachers, or unprepared teachers in low performing schools is bullshit. Teaching is a craft. It cannot rely on quick fix practices if the educational system is to be successful.

The "Too Nice Theory" teacher is an example of what happens when a teacher is not prepared, afraid of offending students or setting boundaries and refuses to emulate more seasoned veterans. Rules, expectations and protocols are established in classes that promote discussion and learning. Order has to be established in a class before learning can take place. I am not quite sure what denotes being "too nice", but I came back to a class with students hanging off the rafters. I wanted to find out what could be done differently so this phenomenon did not happen again.

Educational Theories and Theorists

There are multiple theories and theorists when it comes to

classroom management; they include John Dewey, B.F. Skinner, Alfie Kohn, Rudolf Dreikurs, Fredrick Jones, Albert Bandura, William Glasser, Edward Ford, Jean Piaget, The Cantors, Gordon Thomas, Jacob Kounins, The Applied Behavior Analysis, Rudolf Dreikurs and Alfie Kohn. [15]

For African Americans, there is Booker T. Washington, W.E.B. DuBois, Dr. James Comer, African Centered Education, Ruby Payne with Understanding Poverty and Geneva Gay and Culturally Responsive Pedagogy.

School systems include the standard public school district, independent schools, private schools, charter schools and home schooling. There are numerous teacher programs that include the traditional four year college or university model. Non-traditional teaching programs for individuals who crave a career change, and of course post graduate programs like Teach for America or TNTP Teaching Fellows.

So my recruitment message is as follows: **"If you want to become an educator, there are many paths to get to that destination."** And since there are hundreds of paths to achieve your goal of teaching, there are just as many theories on how to be an effective classroom manager.

Many of the suggestions I read do not talk about the role of discipline in the classroom. They encourage teachers to play games, become a part of the classroom, move around and build relationships with students from different races and cultures without providing a structure on how to create relevant and appropriate boundaries.

It is impossible to read all of the literature on classroom management. There are new management tricks advertised daily. As a twelve year veteran, I find each year brings new challenges on creating successful students. There are a few things that remain constant. I assist my students in creating class rules. I set expectations for them and show them examples on what it looks like to be successful. I model protocols on how I want them to operate in my class, and I insist they are respectful and positive towards each other and me. If I have done this correctly, we as a class start to build a rapport. It is during this time learning can take place. Building relationships with students is equally as important as what I teach. Positive relationships and learning go hand in hand.

Are you an alpha or are you a beta?

When a teacher refuses to be the leader in a class, then another leader will arise. Or as my dad says, "When a vacuum exists, SOMETHING will fill it up." As the teacher in a class of eager students waiting to learn, I am responsible for being the leader in the classroom. If not, there is another person, usually an alpha student, ready and willing to take my place. I chose this profession. I went to school, paid good money, passed my classes, interviewed and purchased additional school supplies to become a professional educator so I need to act like one.

Professionally, it is incumbent upon me to be educationally ready, instructionally sound and capable of building relationships that encourage lifelong learning. That means planning, planning, planning. My lesson plans should be filled with more information than a student can complete in one period. My countenance should remain authentic yet calm. It is important for me to be more learned in my subject matter than my students; yet, be able to receive information from a student when it is new and relevant.

As the teacher, it does not matter if I am in my regular classroom, substituting for another staff member or providing a bathroom break, it is important that my presence continues to provide a safe and manageable classroom. Is this hard for a new teacher, or substitute... absolutely. But it can be done. It is done when the culture of the school expects this type of classroom management and encourages teachers to enlist their students in making a respectful environment the norm instead of an anomaly. So, what happens when you leave your classroom in the hands of a colleague who does not share your same type class discipline? Personally, it is fine with me, as long as they have some type of discipline policy. The fact that a teacher can be perceived as being "too nice" is a problem worth looking in to. To me, it stems from how our students perceive themselves, and the sub-culture that says "nice guys finish last". For our young people, it is often more popular to present a fake façade of toughness than one of kindness. Being disrespectful, speaking unkindly, rudeness and being impolite are learned behaviors.

It takes thick skin to weather many phrases students use when addressing teachers. Teachers who are invested in responding "tit for tat" to a student's learned behavior find they are demoralized and saddened. I am not sure if this type of teacher feels like they are not making a difference, or if they are ineffective? Being concerned whether a student likes you or not weighs so heavily on a teachers mind. If what you are doing is enforcing expectations then that will help your students grow academically and keep them safe.

Was I disappointed in my students when I returned to class? The answer is yes. I had a discussion with them again on my expectations. And believe it or not, when I was out later that semester with bronchitis and laryngitis I had one substitute stay for three days.

As a lead teacher, I did speak to my colleague. It is important to speak with co-workers on classroom expectations, and how to do things better next time. Two of the best gifts teachers can give each other is a listening ear, and space for reflection without fear of recrimination. Was I mad? Yes. Not only at the students, I was mad at my coworker too. However, I got over it. He deserved the same grace I offer my students. He was caught off guard, and my savvy 12 and 13 year-olds smelled blood and took advantage. In the end, it was a learning experience for all of us. And isn't that what school is all about. Learning comes in many forms. The "too nice" teacher, my class of students and I, all learned a lesson that day.

Reflection Notes

What is your story?

_____

_____

_____

_____

_____

_____

_____

_____

_____

_____

_____

_____

_____

_____

_____

_____

_____

_____

_____

Reflection Notes

Websites and Articles:

1. _____

2. _____

3. _____

4. _____

5. _____

6. _____

7. _____

Institution, District or Local Resources:

1. _____

2. _____

3. _____

4. _____

5. _____

6. _____

7. _____

Reflection Notes

Action Plan: _____

Date: _____

_____

_____

_____

_____

_____

_____

_____

_____

_____

_____

_____

_____

_____

_____

_____

_____

_____

_____

Chapter 4 -

"It's food stamp day...so I will not be here tomorrow!"

Holidays are times when my student's exhibit mixed emotions. They are happy to be out of school for a few days. They are disheartened to be out of school for a few days. In discussing the Thanksgiving break, one of my students yells out that she will not be there the next day. When asked why, she plainly states, "It's food stamp day...so I will not be here tomorrow!" She went on to explain her mother needed her to go grocery shopping with her and they would be getting their food stamps, so she was going with her mom the next day.

I could have castigated her, I could have talked about the value of her education and how important it was for her to be in school every day, or I could have embarrassed her with my attitude stemming from my middle class privilege and told her that "we" don't discuss those type of things in class. Instead, I found it to be a lesson in trust.

My student trusted me, and her classmates to state that she was on government assistance and stamps played a vital role in her family. Yes, I missed my student the next day. She explained her planned absence in advance and made it back prior to break; satisfied her family had a house full of food.

"Low or very low food insecurity" is the most current term used when discussing a household that does not have enough food for sustenance. According to the United States Department of Agriculture (USDA), beginning in 2005 the definition of food insecurity is:

• **Low food security** (*old label=Food insecurity without hunger):* reports of reduced quality, variety, or desirability of diet. Little or no indication of reduced food intake.

Very low food security (*old label=Food insecurity with hunger*): Reports of multiple indications of disrupted eating patterns and reduced food intake.

In 2015, the percentage of U.S. households with children that exhibited some level of food insecurity was 16.6%.[16] The national average of households that experienced low food security was 14%. Various subsets exist within these numbers:

> Households with children headed by a single woman (30.3 percent),
>
> Households with children headed by a single man (22.4 percent),
>
> Black, non-Hispanic households (21.5%),
>
> Hispanic households (19.1%), and
>
> Low-income households with incomes below 185 percent of the poverty threshold (32.8%; the Federal poverty line was $24,036 for a family of four in 2015).[17]

In addition to a shortage of household food, students in urban and rural areas are often subjected to living in food deserts: this is an area where there is little or no access to "fresh, healthy, and affordable food".[18] Convenience stores or small markets are the norm in these areas, as opposed to large grocery stores, super stores like Wal-Mart or Target, or super markets.

When teaching in urban districts, the likelihood of teaching students who suffer from some level of low food security is high. In the past, when a student's family were recipients of the governments Supplemental Nutrition Assistance Program (SNAP), what we in the "hood" called food stamps, there was a negative stigma attached. In order to cut down on fraud, the illegal selling of food stamps and to assist in running a more economically efficient program, most families who receive SNAP benefits are provided an EBT or Electronic Benefit

Transfer card, (what looks like a debit card). Consequently, when purchasing groceries you cannot tell one credit or debit card user from another.

Still, families that receive these benefits are often plagued by stigmas attached to being he beneficiaries of government programs. When I googled "stigmas attached to receiving SNAP benefits" there were over 54,000 responses. News articles, essays, television news segments that list various reasons why some qualified families did not want to apply for the SNAP program.

In my neighborhood, being on government assistance is not shameful. My student proudly announced that her mama was taking her shopping because their food stamp card would be replenished. I don't know what type of groceries they bought. Nor do I pretend to know what was considered where her household fit on the hunger safety net spectrum; I do know that after her declaration, several other students stated the dates their families received benefits, and we took a few minutes to have a quick class discussion about the importance of food. This was not so much a teachable moment for me, but I valued the openness of this group to discuss a once taboo subject out loud.

My mother used to tell me that she didn't realize they (her family) was poor. She grew up in a small town and everyone lived the same way. When measured to the national standards of the day, my grandparents probably did not have a lot of money. What my mother did have, and what my parents provided for my brother and myself, was security. I never worried about a place to sleep, food on the table or transportation. I always felt safe. In that classroom, students were secure and willing to "air their laundry" because they looked around and saw their friends, who looked and lived in a similar way.

Hunger, poverty, despair, drugs, mental illness, homelessness, poor credit, no money, unworthiness, undervalued represents a tiny list of issues my kids face on a daily basis. Of course, there were families who were doing well. There are always families that do well. Students who had two parent households and lived in houses with mortgages. The school where I taught had several families who defied the statistics of the zip code in which they lived. Still, the majority of my students did not come from this environment. Most were struggling.

The Money Gap

So, how does a teacher like me, raised middle-class, build relationships with students who live in poverty or low income settings? My answer: with deliberate intent. I worked in several schools with this issue. One year, a high school where I taught had twenty-one Teach For America (TFA) teachers. Young people who recently graduated from college and had applied and been accepted to teach in an inner city school district. The idea that 21 and 22 year olds with a summers worth of teacher training could be an asset to a school is beyond what I believe, but that is discussion for another day. One of my mother's favorite sayings was, "when life gives you lemons, make lemonade".

In my teaching career, I have had two excellent principals, and three that were not great to me; but I learned from them also. In the high school with the large number of TFA's, I was blessed with a smart, proactive, diligent, outspoken and administratively shrewd principal, who led by example. Ms. Collins worked with her staff in a collaborative manner. She allowed and encouraged the veteran staff to build relationships and work with our new recruits. These young people were fish out of water. We were tasked with helping them rise to the challenge of working in one of the most crime ridden, poverty-stricken neighborhoods in Kansas City.

In modeling what a staff should do with their students, the district assigned each new teachers a mentor. As mentors, we were tasked with building relationships with our young staff. One of the ways we bonded was by introducing our teachers to Kansas City. We had spirited conversations after work, went to happy hour, met for dinner and got to know a little more about each other. The relationships we developed went from superficial niceties to long enduring bonds. The new teachers brought a refreshing attitude of "nothing is impossible" and we encouraged them to merge their "can do" spirit with rituals and routines that had proven to be successful with our students. The majority of the new group was receptive, and the ones that were hold outs, we let flounder. As with students, some folks have to learn lessons in a different way.

During this period, three of us wrote and presented a professional development (PD) workshop to our associates. Our team consisted of a male TFA from New York City, and two established teachers. We called it the "64128 Series". Using inspiration from Yale University's Dr. James Comer, using information from Ruby Payne's "A Framework for Understanding Poverty" we data mined zip code statistics from the 2010 census. This information allowed us to create a compelling presentation on why teachers have difficulty in building relationships with students who are different.

Our workshop did not shy away from issues regarding race, income disparity, hunger, homelessness, the educability of our students, and our personal use of disposable income. We started by comparing the base salary of starting teachers in our district to the average income of a family of four from the three main zip codes where our students lived. The data showed a $12,000 gap between a single teacher's pay and a family of four. This knowledge set the tone for the rest of our workshop. We discussed formal and informal registers of language, personal bias awareness, community building in the classroom, and the role the teacher has in instituting policies of equity, instead of trying to treat everyone as being equal.

It was an exhausting and satisfying day. Using a personal psychological platform which says most people respond to controversial information from someone that looks similar, our young TFA introduced many of the challenging topics. He used his personal reaction to the information as the catalyst for leading his part of the discussion. By stating some changes he was willing to make in his teaching strategies, he opened the door for others to ask questions, voice opinions and provide suggestions on how to personally and collectively move the school forward.

The reaction to our presentation was overwhelmingly positive. Of course, there were naysayers. Individuals who decided not to be reflective or make adjustments to how they could do things differently: I leave this group alone. Many teachers expressed it was one of the best school workshops they had attended. Of course, my co-workers did an excellent job and we all played to our strengths. What we were most proud about was introducing a controversial topic to a skeptical group in a non-threatening way.

As a teacher, part of my job is to read between the lines of what a kid says, and what they mean. Many of my colleagues take statements that students say personally. My student who told me that she would be grocery shopping with her mother instead of coming to school clearly articulated what was important to her family. I would have been more concerned if her voice cracked in desperation, or she intimated she was hungry or that her house had no food. It is not what a kid says, but how it is said that dictates the seriousness of a situation. Don't be afraid to ask questions. If one particular teacher feels uncomfortable digging deeper into a student's conversation, ask for assistance.

A student is usually close to at least one teacher. I would love to walk into the teacher's lounge and hear them discuss helping students instead of talking about students negatively. It takes a few minutes to find the teacher who has a relationship with a specific challenging student. Students typically reach out to one teacher who makes them feel visible. Educators who shape relationships with unpleasant or disagreeable students can assist in finding solutions to reach students who are difficult to work with. By communicating and proactively working together, teachers can create a less isolated environment when managing challenging students.

I have witnessed teachers sneak food to students who exhibit signs of hunger. I'm guilty of keeping extra food in my desk drawer and refrigerator in case a student tells me they are have not eaten. I watch students scarf down food in the cafeteria, and ask their fellow students for leftovers. I watch the kid that gets skinnier and gaunt during the school year. Overcoming food insecurity is vital in increasing student achievement.

Why is Breakfast Important?

Research confirms that breakfast is the most important meal of the day for children's health, academic achievement, cognitive development and mental health. Unfortunately, many children regularly skip breakfast each morning, depriving them of the important benefits associated with the morning meal. In fact, though most schools in the United States offer the School Breakfast Program, less than a quarter of all students and less than half of the students who are eligible for a free or reduced price breakfast are eating it. [18]

A well-nourished scholar is the first step in the long process of increased student achievement. There are plenty of models for schools that choose to build relationships with local food banks. There are specific agencies that provide food for students to take home daily or weekly basis. In the cafeteria, a second helping can be given to students who are hungry until the daily allotment of lunch has been exhausted. If you are looking for ideas, google and review websites, visit different school programs and check with your local churches and food banks for ideas and information on alleviating hunger in your community.

When a student is comfortable in class, they stop comparing their reality to their teacher's. In unguarded moments, students offer insight into their way of life outside of school. Listen closely. Use these situations as teachable moments. If you, the teacher, are unsure of your students' intentions, call your pupil forward and quietly ask, "What is going on?" Don't run from unfamiliar or difficult topics. We all have the capacity to learn from each other, and in the process create an environment that builds bridges and communicates respect to produce thoughtful young adults.

Reflection Notes

What is your story?

_____

_____

_____

_____

_____

_____

_____

_____

_____

_____

_____

_____

_____

_____

_____

_____

_____

_____

_____

_____

_____

Reflection Notes

Websites and Articles:

1. _____

2. _____

3. _____

4. _____

5. _____

6. _____

7. _____

Institution, District or Local Resources:

1. _____

2. _____

3. _____

4. _____

5. _____

6. _____

7. _____

Reflection Notes

Action Plan: _____

Date: _____

_____

_____

_____

_____

_____

_____

_____

_____

_____

_____

_____

_____

_____

_____

_____

_____

_____

_____

_____

Chapter 5 –

OMG - The school mascot is under house arrest

During a rally for mandatory state testing, our school mascot takes the stage to chants and cheers. One of my students turns to me and asks "why is the school mascot wearing an ankle monitor?" I seek out the coach over the event and point out the obvious. Five minutes later, the mascot was off the stage and the rally continued.

All of the urban schools where I have worked had a small group of students who were processing through the juvenile court system. As a teacher, this realization was sobering. I was not prepared to teach students who were labeled "juvenile delinquents". My other kids were numb to their classmates and friends who wore ankle monitoring devices and those who had been detained or arrested for various legal infractions. In fact, this small group was quite popular.

Juvenile offenders typically wore some type of monitoring system and had to attend school as a condition of their parole. Ankle monitors use Global Positioning System (GPS) technology to track the location of the wearer. Monitors that are not charged correctly constantly beep, and can disrupt a quiet learning environment. This presents a challenge in classroom seating arrangements since these students need to sit near a wall socket. I have seen high schoolers brazenly walk the hallways with their monitor cord around their necks as a status symbol. I asked myself, "What in the hell was I going to do with a kid who obviously didn't care about the law?", and how do I teach him or her?"

According to the U.S. Department of Justice and the U.S. Department of Education, "There are more than 60,000 young people in the juvenile justice residential facilities in the United States on any given day."[19] The Campaign for Youth Justice states "Every year, juvenile courts in the U.S. handle an estimated 1.7 million cases in which the youth was charged with a delinquency offense, approximately 4,600 delinquency cases per day."[20]

Zero tolerance policies, or strict enforcement of school rules and codes in order to restrict undesirable behaviors, became prevalent in 1994. H.R. 6 Improving America's Schools Act created a zero tolerance policy and was designed to keep schools gun free. The Improving America's Schools Act passed in October of 1994. The Guns-Free School Act is a part of the legislation enacted at that time and spelled out the consequences of bringing a firearm into a school.

"The GFSA states that each State receiving Federal funds under [Elementary and Secondary Education Act of 1965] ESEA must have in effect, by October 20, 1995, a State law requiring local educational agencies to expel from school **for a period of not less than one year a student who is determined to have brought a weapon to school.** *Each State's law also must allow the chief administering officer of the local educational agency (LEA) to modify the expulsion requirement on a case-by-case basis."*[21]

The history of school violence runs wide and deep in America. On the website www.k12academics.com, there is a listing of school violence that dates to the 1700's. It has a detailed listing of school incidents from colonial days until 2010. On the conservative website www.ballotpedia.com, there is an overview of school shootings that have taken place from 1990 and is updated regularly.

Gun violence is the one act that gets the most press. Each time a shooting takes place in a school, college or university, the media covers it from coast to coast. This is not to diminish the severity of gun violence. I teach students who are on the road to incarceration as young as age 10. I am simply concerned with how easy it is for a young person to obtain a gun in any community.

The truth is simple, it can be downright scary to teach in an urban school. In order to work in a school, I had to go through a rigorous background check to secure my job. When applying at a district, a teacher surrenders all rights to privacy. Our fingerprints are even placed on file with the FBI. We typically pay to have someone review our previous positions and whether or not we have broken the law or are a registered sex offender. This requirement for employment is what each teacher has to take into account if they are to pursue a career in education.

Numbers Don't Lie

So, who is responsible for training teachers when they are confronted with possible violent offenders? School districts mandate a teacher pass a mandatory background check to work in a school with the prospect of teaching students who are processing through the justice system. If you are a new teacher, or a person who has had little interaction with the law, then you are at a loss on how to work with kids who are in the cycle of incarceration. When most of your dealings with law enforcement have been positive, you have no understanding of how a student so young could run afoul the law, and the people sworn and paid to protect their rights.

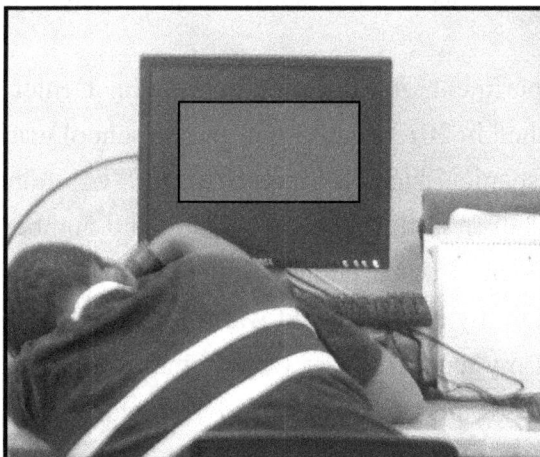

Statistically speaking, white people in the United States have more confidence in police officers than their black counterparts.

Confidence in Police

	A Great Deal/ Quite a Lot	Some	Very Little/None
	%	%	%
National Adults	56	30	14
White	59	29	12
Black	37	37	28
Gallup poll aggregate from surveys conducted in June 2011, June 2012, June 2013 and June 2014[22]			

This group includes my fellow staff members who are primarily white. Teachers who are new to the urban core are often in "shock and awe" after the first few weeks of school. You hear their bewilderment in coded statements such as, "These students are really loud", "Hmmm, I wonder where he or she got their name from?" And the inevitable, "I don't think their parent cares anything about him or her, otherwise he or she wouldn't have gotten into trouble." All true statements spoken to me as if because I am Black, I had some magical insight into a student's home.

The Department of Education's National Center for Education Statistics published in 2013 that 82% of public school teachers are white, 7% are non-Hispanic Black, 8% are Hispanic. The number of female teachers was 76% versus 24% male for the overall number[23]. Simply put, the average student in the United States public school system will probably be taught by a 40 year old white female. Don't get me wrong. The majority of my teachers were white females; but I had a mama and daddy that put a tremendous amount of importance on education. My brother and I were not allowed to act like fools at school. Rest assured, we believed there were spies everywhere, lurking around every corner, waiting to dial my parents number the minute we looked as if we were going to get out of control.

I overhear my older colleagues talk nostalgically about the good old days. From my point of view, school has always been riddled with strife. There have always been "juvenile delinquents" who attended public school. Whether it was the student who played pranks on other students, the playground bully, the girls and boys that smoked cigarettes in the bathroom, or the couple caught kissing under the bleachers. It's easy to romanticize about the school days of yore, but schools are just a microcosm of the community. The good old days reflect the society of the time, when schools were homogenous and folks didn't have to worry about crossing the cultural divide.

Nonetheless, my parents who were Black, went to segregated schools and all of their peers and teachers were black. After 1954, the schools were ordered to be segregated but not the staff. Where "negro or colored" schools had Black staff, administrators and faculty, "integrated" schools did not make it a priority to desegregate teachers or administration. Values, traditions and beliefs considered important in Black communities were not significant to schools with a smattering of black students.

The Same, but Different

In the olden days, there was no internet or social media to contend with. As a technology teacher, I contend with the "1 to 1 learning initiative". This is an idea to put a laptop in the hands of every student. This noble idea should not be implemented without safe guards. Under the cloak on anonymity, students speak ill of each other, girls and boys are sought out and groomed by internet predators, and inappropriate websites are procured and shared without oversight. Teachers put up with a lot of shit these days that is quite simply out of their control.

If we are to assist new and experienced teachers with classroom management and ways to cope with socially connected students of all types, we have to create professional development and training that provides substantive tools to overcome these encounters. Student challenges run the gamut from affluent to homeless. The thing all students have in common are none of them want to appear stupid in the eyes of their teacher or classmates. Students who are walking around with monitoring equipment have an established reputation. Often, in the urban core, this student is looked up to as a hero or a person to emulate.

From what I have seen and heard, teachers who go into urban schools with the attitude they are going to save the world burn out quickly. The enthusiasm and exuberance brought to teaching is replaced with disappointment when met with school and district policies. I will never forget the young teacher that when told by the principal our school had $2000.00 for field trips, he quickly calculated how many students could go and stated the number he would like to invite, which took up the total budget. She looked at him incredulously and stated, "That was the budget for the whole school, for the whole year." The teacher was ticked off, the principal was irritated, and the reality of working in the urban core instantly became real.

Educators in high poverty schools have to look at things differently. Students are different. The circumstances in which students come to school daily are different. The family make up is different. Access to disposable income is different. The diet is different. What is important is different. EVERYTHING is different. On the other hand, different does not denote bad. It means being realistic about what is available and operating out of the hope and aspiration that students desire a positive school experience. Students in high needs schools want the same things as other students: they want to be safe. Students want to learn and these kids want access to technology.

But when asked, the first thing most students say they want is respect. I have talked with hundreds of kids, and the word "respect" is often the first thing out of their mouths. I always ask the follow-up question, "What does that mean?" I am met with shrugged shoulders and mumbled comments that they're not sure what that means. I press harder. What I have learned is that students are scared of being vulnerable. In the schools, the harder you look and act, the more respect you earn. In a classroom, the opposite is true. The more defiant you present yourself in a class, the higher likelihood you are of being labeled a trouble maker. Other students might think you are comical, or that you "got that teacher told". In reality, students are building a negative reputation, typically one from which they cannot recover. As a Black or Hispanic child, once you are labeled as a difficult student, the return to respectability is a "hard row to hoe".

This not only happens with children, but it can happen with a family name. Everyone in a neighborhood knows a family that is branded rotten. As kids, you are told to stay away from a particular house and its inhabitants. Teachers shudder when they know that a student from "that" family will be placed in their class. The negative tattoo of undesirability for all members from specific household is set in stone. In a Black church, this is referred to as a generational curse. In a school system, these students are pegged as bad kids from bad families.

Starting the school year with a mentally clean slate towards all assigned students is a great way for a teacher to start a new school year. Putting aside negative conversations and comments about a school's reputation offers room for a teacher to create their own setting for student engagement. Providing a safe classroom is one way to produce a positive environment for students who have been negatively labeled.

A reading teacher talked about the importance of building community in the classroom during a professional development session I was attending. She specifically stated it was the responsibility of the teacher to take time to craft a safe environment. By discussing with students procedures on how to talk and act during learning activities, she was able to set the parameters of what was acceptable behavior. This conversation with her classes held at the beginning of the school year set the tone for the whole year. Students who are outliers (those who have broken the law or in the throes of the system) are provided a fresh start when all students start the year on equal footing with their classmates.

When a student is wearing a GPS monitor in class, set him or her close to an outlet to provide the student dignity. The instructor is responsible for taking away the mystique and informal sense of power a labeled student has in class by placing the student in a position where they cannot gain control of the course. Recalling Adolescent Psychology, provide a clean slate to students on a daily basis. As the leader in the classroom, I have learned not to burden myself with retribution against students whom I don't like, or who are raised differently than I. The truth is, there will always be students who are more challenging, and come to you with problems and issues that seem insurmountable. It is important to model the behavior that you want your students to display. This takes hard work, it takes practice and it takes patience. Perseverance with students and forgiving resilience for oneself keeps effective teachers coming back year after year. The belief that I can make a difference keeps me teaching.

The reality is clear, educators in all communities will have students in their class who are a part of the legal system. We have students who come from negatively stereotyped families. We have students who are literally homeless, and those who travel from couch to couch. Students whose young livelihoods are disrupted are more prone to struggle with the constraints of a school setting. There will be students we like better than others, and kids that demonstrate negative characteristics.

The bottom line is that these students deserve the same respect and deference we offer our "good" students. If we cannot provide services to our kids that need it the most, then schools should rethink their role in today's society. The "good old days" are gone. If we choose the profession of teaching, then we have made the choice to work with these children also.

Positive parameters work; not pity, disappointment or shame. Every district should be open to individual schools adopting comprehensive and meaningful classroom management systems that pertain to a particular school's demographic. Each system should encourage teachers to reward positive behavior and work with students who exhibit destructive conduct. Utilizing interventionists, family, community and religious organizations widen the circle of safety to help students understand their eventual role in society. The introduction of outside sources offers all students additional voices in helping them grow to become successful adults.

Young lawbreakers are going to be a part of the school system as long as the law requires youth to attend public school. I reject the notion that a teacher without support from administrators and district personnel can change the trajectory of a hardened student. I do believe with proper supports, behavior specialists, open communication and dialogue the educational community can address the concern teachers have regarding juveniles who are in the legal system and come up with better solutions than what are currently in place. This to me is tantamount to looking the other way, instead of addressing teacher concerns.

Schools that embrace restorative justice principles at the elementary and middle school level often see a decrease in school suspensions. I was not a true believer until I took a five week course in conflict resolution. It took the first three weeks until I bought into the principles of restorative justice. Because of my conversion, I have aligned myself with the Center for Conflict Resolution in Kansas City, Mo. They work with students on anger management, impulse control and other social emotional tools to assist student in properly venting their frustration. This organization works with small groups of students, and don't get bothered by the initial rejection students often display in the first meeting. This is just one avenue to work with students who are identified by the legal community.

There are countless articles and studies on restorative justice practices in the educational setting. A school or staff do not have to be experts in the field. Administrators and teachers have to be open to trying something new in order to get different results. By using training, empathy, role play and a professional team that can teach the staff during professional development sessions, provides a few answers to teaching students who are in the correctional system, and those who are on their way.

It takes an inordinate amount of energy to concentrate on the 5 – 12% of students who are identified as the most challenging in a public school. An proactive administrative and teacher team who enact a plan, encourage constant contact with parents, guardians and caseworkers and show respect and empathy for this population can make a difference. A school has to be honest about the population they serve. Only then can a true plan be put into place to make a difference in each child's life, regardless of their status or station in the school.

Reflection Notes

What is your story?

_____

_____

_____

_____

_____

_____

_____

_____

_____

_____

_____

_____

_____

_____

_____

_____

_____

_____

_____

Reflection Notes

Websites and Articles:

1. _____

2. _____

3. _____

4. _____

5. _____

6. _____

7. _____

Institution, District or Local Resources:

1. _____

2. _____

3. _____

4. _____

5. _____

6. _____

7. _____

Reflection Notes

Action Plan: _____

Date: _____

_____

_____

_____

_____

_____

_____

_____

_____

_____

_____

_____

_____

_____

_____

_____

_____

_____

_____

Me and My Mama's Tattoo

Chapter 6 -

2 x 3 = 4

As an In School Suspension instructor, students who are sent to me are often provided assignments from their teachers. A young student was in my class and having trouble on a pre-algebra assignment. This young lady was a 13, soon to be 14 year old 7th grader. Her assignment involved solving for y with an x variable, ex: 2x-1=y. She was given the numbers 0, 2, 3 and 6 in the x column. She solved for y relatively easily when the x was 0, but when I asked her to multiply 2 x 3, she answered 4. I told her that was incorrect, and she immediately asked for a calculator, to which I said no.

Her teacher was next door, and when I asked him about her need for a calculator on such a simple task, he informed me that according to the district policy and his math coach, it was decided it was more important for the students to learn the concept than to know their multiplication tables. Of course I argued the point. I asked about math drills at the beginning of class, homework assignments, and anything that would assist the students who were struggling with multiplication to memorize the times table.

*After much discussion, I looked at him incredulously and I tersely asked, "So, this would be good enough for **your** child?" To his credit, he didn't answer me, he looked pissed and walked out of my class, then I gave that student a calculator.*

I have always worked in urban school setting. It is by personal design that I have aligned myself with urban education. Although I am a product of laboratory, black neighborhood, all white suburban and magnet schools, my parents and teachers have always expected me to do my best from day one. Back in the day, I didn't realize I was doing anything different. Most of my friends were competitive, and we all tried to be the smartest one in the class. I didn't think it unusual to be considered a top student. So it came a surprise to me as I started getting older to find many of my peers did not revere school the same why I did.

I benefited from parents that prized education. Growing up, I thought ALL parents gave their children flash cards, board games and puzzles to encourage critical thinking. I believed that most of my friends did crossword puzzles and had times table relays. I assumed that the discussions at the dinner table centered on what you learned at school that day, and how to make the next day more challenging. Damn, was I wrong! There were some of my friends who were raised in a similar fashion, but looking back, I realize most of them were TK's (teacher's kids). In fact, it wasn't until I was much older that I realized I was probably the odd man out.

Because I realized that white or black, blue, green or yellow, not all kids have the same learning opportunities, the disparities show up in the classroom. It became vitally important for me to always be prepared and smarter than my students. At least in the subject area I taught.

In order to make my classroom come alive, I have to be fully knowledgeable of my students' capabilities, the curriculum, and learning targets. As an instructor I am accountable for planning informative lessons based upon test objectives. I had to learn that I could only test a student on what I had taught, not what I wanted them to learn, or what they should have learned before. If my students were behind, whether I liked it or not, I was the one responsible for getting them caught up.

If I don't have the proper records to evaluate my students, then I am responsible for pre-testing my students, so I am aware and I understand their deficits. I don't have time to bellyache about what my students shoulda, woulda or coulda known. We all have an idea of where we want our students to be academically, emotionally and socially when they enter the classroom. Let me save you a headache: throw away all of our preconceived notions and work with what you have. Quit bitching about where you think your students should be, take them where they are. Then help them rise.

The fact that it was ok for a capable 13 year-old girl not to know her multiplication facts made me sick! I cannot imagine where this would be acceptable; but, in an urban school setting for some reason, we have been led to believe the mediocre is magical, and the marginal is great. I constantly say, "Teaching is hard work." When we have low expectations of students, they always meet that low goal.

My friends who teach core subjects lament the lack of rote memorization that is not taught in the lower grades. My math teacher peers are pissed off that students have not been required to learn their times tables. English teachers are not happy about a student's lack of understanding the parts of speech, the use of prepositional phrases, vocabulary and writing a basic sentence. Social studies teachers have to teach the list of presidents and the three branches of government year after year because students are not able to recall this basic information. Science teachers don't trust students with Bunsen burners, test tubes and basic chemicals so classes don't do experiments in the middle schools I have taught.

There is a national discussion brewing about the deficiency of advanced and AP courses at high schools in urban neighborhoods. Funding for field trips is low, so administrators are hesitant to use school funds on buses. Teachers don't have faith that their kids will act properly on school outings, so they are reluctant to ask, and when they do, the field trip is required to be tied to the curriculum.

What ever happened to various grades going to the local museum, the symphony, local playhouses and the park? One of the major components of a wonderful education stems from exposure.

Students who participate in activities that give them information outside of their traditional areas of comfort excel.

Going to summer school for enrichment was how I grew up. We never went to summer school to make up grades. I went to take an advanced science class in 8th grade. Taking additional coursework in the summer allowed me to go to school half a day my senior year of high school.

In the last three schools I have worked, students who are in danger of not going to the next grade are identified in the third quarter. These are kids who have low attendance rates or who have had 4 or more failing grades in their core subjects during the first three quarters. In order for Johnny to go to the next grade, he will have to attend summer school and pass all of these classes. I believe students who are in jeopardy of failing can be recognized within the first grading period.

Test scores from the previous year are distributed during the first three weeks of school. Using this data provides the administrative team and staff with a road map on identifying the scholars who the most help. Students who are on grade level can continue to work at their assigned pace. Those students need more assistance can be provided with intervention strategies at the beginning of the year. As they meet and exceed expectations, this group can graduate to the next level. Scholars who need additional help can continue to receive it from assigned staff.

These are the conversations the teachers I know have when discussing student achievement. They desire students come to them ready. And my co-workers get angry when they are pointed to as the reason why test scores are low. Knowing how to use auto correct, spell check and a calculator is not the answer for kids who are already behind. Students must be provided with skills to read, think, interpret, analyze and communicate.

Stern is the new Black

The question remains, how do I take students who are behind and help them attain grade level status? Some of it is back to basic teaching: strict and flexible approach with high expectations. In today's school settings it appears that if the students don't love you, you are ineffective. When I was in school for my administrative credentials, one of our biggest discussions centered on a question asked from the professor, "Do you have to love the students you teach?"

I don't believe in embarrassing students, but I will call them out for their inappropriate behavior. Dr. Rita Pierson, in her famous TED Talk "Every kid needs a champion" states she once heard a colleague say, "They don't pay me to like the kids." Her response, "Kids don't learn from people they don't like."[24] I wholeheartedly agree with Dr. Pierson; but, I would like to add, students don't learn from teachers they don't respect either.

In the classroom, the teacher is the ADULT, period. One of my favorite professional development sessions centered on learning Kagan strategies. Kagan Cooperative Learning strategies are various ways teachers can employ social interactions in the class to facilitate learning through team building. I was most impressed by the instructor, who when going over norms for our adult group, stated that she explains to her students she was the "Queen" of the classroom and they were princes and princesses. She never referred to her students as her royal subjects, or anything that was subordinate, but worked with them on their responsibilities as children that were privy to all the rights of a royal family. By announcing she was the Queen, she proclaimed she was the adult in the room, but she also gave her students space to be students. She provided a platform of success because she provided a safe, fun and expectation rich environment for her students. It was her job to explain what a prince and princess looked like in her class, and hold her students to their roles.

However you address your students, the role in which you place yourself in the classroom speaks volumes to how you value yourself as a teacher. I often say, "If my friends are twelve and thirteen (middle school aged children), I might have a problem." If I present myself as a caring adult who has expectations and procedures that are rooted in boundaries and mutual respect, I have a much better chance of being successful.

When I merge my expectations and procedures with the curriculum knowledge I possess, I present a professionally certified teacher who has an aspiration of seeing students thrive. My promise to my students is and always will be that, "You will be a smarter person when you exit my class, than when you entered." I use my **Shipley Brand** of modeling and instruction to encourage my students to become learned and productive citizens in the class and school.

I realize all of my students may not like me, but for the most part, they respect me. When I said to my father, "There are some students I can't reach" he explained to me that if I reach one, then I have done my job. It was my obligation to plant seeds, it might be someone else who waters them and sees them grow. Again, my familial **tattoo** superseded the advice of the experts, and allows me to live within reasonable expectations with extraordinary results.

Proudly, I follow in my mother's footsteps. Just as her students and professional peers remembered the outstanding teacher, counselor, principal and friend during her funeral services, I too have embarked on a legacy of service. I too have former students who seek me out to say thank you. I have peers and co-workers who value my opinion. I have former bosses and principles who allow me to tap their expertise and engage in verbal jousting. Still, my perceived sternness often leaves new teachers and those who are not African American perplexed.

That was the case with this young man who wholeheartedly swallowed the district policy of teaching a concept versus helping students learn using comprehension and memorization skills, in addition to the new methods of instruction. There is a lot of good stuff in new teaching strategies. But we cannot dismiss the old, just because we have new technological toys like IPADS, laptops, computers labs graphing calculators and games.

We have yet to see the impact technology has on brain development. It is well-known the value of reading, memorization, the use of flash cards and the role language acquisition plays in helping to map the brain. With technology, we are required to use the new tools, and I think they should be a part of the learning process. I wonder what would happened if we combined the two concepts? If students in lower levels went back to a basic education formula, and in the fourth or fifth grade, start combining their learned skills with technology and hand held devices, then I believe we could raise student achievement. Young people today already have a clear sense of how to use cell phones and computerized items, we can extend that knowledge by assisting them in how to use these tools to their best abilities.

As a seasoned teacher, it is important I extend an olive branch to new and younger educators entering the profession. Older teachers have experience and classroom management skills that can be passed on to the next generation. New converts to the profession bring new ideas, energy and computer talents more in tune with our future generation of learners. Together, we can generate combined tactics so all students can learn and be labeled advanced or proficient.

I have been blessed to mentor many new teachers. I keep in contact with approximately eight of these young people. About half have gotten out of the profession and are working in fields that they enjoy. The other four have continued as teachers. We have great conversations about their initial naiveté and what they learned while teaching. I remind my friends that they taught me few things as well. We laugh, we drink and we keep each other posted on our lives. I have grown richer since I have known this new group of friends.

Using tried and true methods, creative energy, an excellent

curriculum and a willingness to keep working with our children can lead to student success. When these methods translate into test scores, the public will take notice. It will take teachers, instructional coaches and administrators who are willing to buck the trick-inspired trends, to speak the truth about what they are experiencing, and prayerfully stay in the profession who will make the difference.

In the pursuit of excellence, we cannot "throw the baby out with the bathwater". It is important our students learn the new, but also develop the skills they will need to have a good job and provide for their families. Black students don't have the same options as their white counterparts. The real issue I have with most top down policies are they are enacted by people who are not in the trenches.

The desired outcome is for all students to be on grade level throughout their educational career. But it negates the reality of poverty, child neglect and abuse, systemic industrial based poisoning (think Flint, Michigan), hunger, uneducated parents, drug abuse, fetal alcohol syndrome and just plain neglect that many students in urban schools experience. The issues do not go away with a sprinkling of a laptop and teachers who are not trained in educational warfare.

Classroom teachers should be asked to participate in the tools that will be most useful and effective for their children, from pre-k through 12th grade. As a teacher, it is important that I participate. When the district asks for my participation in picking out new curriculum, I am required to provide my input. I cannot bitch about anything if I did not do my part in making my voice known, especially when asked.

I understand this young teacher buying into the district line when he provided his student a calculator to multiply simple numbers. It is almost impossible for students to make up a three to four year deficit when they are in middle school. However, it can be done. If this is the hand we in urban schools have been dealt, then we have to be proactive in solving these issues. Egos need to be put aside for the sake of the students. Board of education employees cannot work in isolation when deciding what should take place in a classroom. A conversation with teachers about problems and possible solutions can take place quarterly. Then we can actively evaluate what is working well, and what needs to be revised. Machinery is nice, but it is time to stop testing policies that don't lend themselves to student learning. Instead start teaching fundamentals and building block basics so we can expand our students' knowledge and use of technology in their later years.

Reflection Notes

What is your story?

_____

_____

_____

_____

_____

_____

_____

_____

_____

_____

_____

_____

_____

_____

_____

_____

_____

_____

Reflection Notes

Websites and Articles:

1. _____

2. _____

3. _____

4. _____

5. _____

6. _____

7. _____

Institution, District or Local Resources:

1. _____

2. _____

3. _____

4. _____

5. _____

6. _____

7. _____

Reflection Notes

Action Plan: _____

Date: _____

_____

_____

_____

_____

_____

_____

_____

_____

_____

_____

_____

_____

_____

_____

_____

_____

_____

_____

_____

_____

Chapter 7

Grace

"When the world pushes you to your knees,
You're in the perfect position to pray."

- Rumi

During the Christmas holiday, I was standing in a line that appeared long and running slow. The checkout next to me was open and the young man behind me encouraged me to go to the open line. As I pushed my cart, the cashier quietly says, "Hi, Ms. Shipley." I look up to see a student I taught 8 years ago. A young lady I have often thought about over the years. I greeted her by her name, and asked if I could hug her. She obliged, and just for a brief moment, hugged me tight. Tears came to my eyes, because this was a student I was sure we had lost. I asked how she was doing. She talked about her kids, and smiled throughout the whole transaction.

As she handed me my receipt, I explained how good it was to see her, and that I occasionally thought of her throughout the years. She seemed genuinely pleased, but not surprised. We wished each other happy holidays and I was on my way. Seeing this young lady after all of these years was my favorite present of the Christmas season.

An African proverb says, "It is not what you are called, but what you answer to." My name, Lynne comes from great grandparents, Sherman and Ruby Linn. Bradley, my brother's name comes from my maternal grandparents' surname. My brother's children also have names that reflect our ancestors. My name is embedded in me; tattooed on my soul. Names in the Black community are important. They provide identity and refuge. On the playground, when one is called out of their name, a fight usually ensues.

Growing up in the sixties and seventies, during busing and desegregation, my brother and I were individually addressed by two different teachers as "nigger". I contacted my parents immediately. Not only was I referred to with the most derogatory slur that can be applied to a Black person, I was called a "nigger" by a teacher. As much as it pissed me off, and I wanted to curse in return, I knew to let my people handle things. This is a lesson I try to impart to my students. There are some issues their parents need to handle.

When I began teaching, my mother told me to learn as many names of my students as possible. Mom used to say, "Students remember two types of teachers, the teachers they loved and the ones they hated." She was speaking unsubstantiated wisdom regarding the impact a teacher has on a student's psyche. As a child, my family often lived in the neighborhood my mother taught. She was my brother's kindergarten teacher, and was the principal of family, friends and neighbors. My parents were community institutions. My dad coached, my mother was an educator. Even when we lived in the suburbs, we shopped, worshipped and hung out in areas that were common to their players and students. I would watch as her students ran to her at the grocery store and introduced mom to their families or friends. Afterwards, mom would say, "Children don't speak to you in public if they don't like you." I was always proud of the lives my parents touched, and dreamed of being "famous" like them.

I recall riding my bicycle by the Jones house. Most evenings in the summer my former teacher would be outside tending her roses. If she was in her garden when I rode by, I would stop and speak for a minute. In order, she would ask about my studies, my brother and my parents.

She always told me how proud she was of me, and I would do well. Mrs. Jones had a son Will who ended up homeless. I remember seeing him downtown when I would go to the movies or shopping. I don't know how Will ended up on the streets, or if he was ashamed, but I knew Mrs. Jones and how she always spoke to me. It was important I speak to him and ask how he was doing. I wanted to acknowledge Will, and because of Mrs. Jones, it was important I called him by his name.

I have worked in schools where students have been referred to as scholars, children, students or kiddos. At my current school, the administrative team often refers to students as friends. I understand the rationale in using friendly nouns to address students, yet it rings disingenuous. In all honesty, none of us have teenagers as our friends. There are kids we like and enjoy being around. Some young folks we take special interest in and mentor, but being friends with a teenager when I am an adult teacher or administrator is downright strange. It can come across as sarcastic when students are referred to in this manner over the intercom or on the walkie-talkie.

It seems more genuine to me to address students by their name. If it is the beginning of the school year and you don't know your students, address them as young man or young lady. A wise teacher never uses boy or girl when speaking to a student of color, unless the kid is under the age of six or seven. This is demeaning and smacks of prejudice.

A name signifies respect. It is the initial tattoo. It is what we will be called and what we answer to. I remember watching the Alex Haley movie "Roots" as a child and observing Omoro hold up his son towards the sky and say "Kunta Kinta, behold...the only thing greater than yourself." This was powerful and moving to me as a child. For the first time on television, I was able to relate how to an African naming ritual. Even though it didn't happen to me, I silently prayed I was introduced to the world in this manner when I was named by my parents. Naming ceremonies are sacred in many cultures. And many religions wait anywhere from one to two weeks before naming their child. There is a revered significance in what a baby is named.

A teacher, who remembers their student's names, pays them respect. Respect in urban communities carries as much weight as gold. Showing a young person respect is the first building block in constructing a positive teacher-student relationship. Creating a well-managed classroom environment is equally important as grades and test scores. There is no increased student achievement in a chaotic classroom. Teachers who take the first few weeks to work with students on forming affirmative relationships and connections with their classmates, create credible student connections which can be used during critical times. If a student is in crisis, the bonds formed within the first few weeks of school aid teachers in deescalating negative situations. These relationships assist teachers in gleaning information from a student's friends when their classmate shuts down. There is always a scholar or two who keeps their instructor up to date on the latest happenings in the neighborhood and school. This open channel of communication is central to a well-oiled classroom.

After establishing class norms and protocols, the assigned curriculum can be introduced to students in chunks according to their achievement level. Taking time to get to know your students, coupled with empirical data, provide a roadmap to the possibilities available for the school year. If you have a lot of students who test well and understand the coursework, then you can plan additional activities to augment the curriculum. Students who have tested low or on grade level, can be given supplementary learning opportunities in addition to district coursework in order to help students become more successful scholars. Activities such as project-based learning combined with traditional models of instruction provide an enriched experience and tie together students of various learning styles for a deeper understanding of core concepts.

Getting to know your students likes and dislikes, strengths and weaknesses provides teachers with a plan to unlock a child's potential. Introducing oneself to parents or guardians using an inviting and positive tone at the beginning of the school year widens the circle of caring adults. I have heard parents complain they only hear from a school when their child has done something "bad" or is in trouble. We need to become better at building familial relationships from an affirmative perspective. This can be done with an introductory letter the student has to take home, creating a class newsletter, calling parents or mailing a notecard about the coming school year. Many districts provide teachers with the ability to make classroom or subject matter websites to provide parents and guardians with the latest news. When I started teaching, each new instructor in my district was given "The First Day of School" by Harry Wong. Twelve years later, I still refer to this book when I am looking for ideas on how to build student relationships.

Greeting family members during the honeymoon phase of a new school year builds good will and goes a long way if and when a student begins to display challenging behavior. Many parents are exasperated when their child is judged by his or her past record. This can include discipline records or test scores. I have never met a parent that did not want to see their child succeed. It is from these conversations that we start to understand what a child is tattooed and branded with at home.

When I saw my student at Wal-Mart, and she did me the courtesy of saying hello, I knew that somewhere in her upbringing she was tattooed with the ability to recognize people who were in her corner. As a teacher, I had conversations with her mother. I knew some of her background, and I knew why she was suspended from school and eventually left altogether. From what I was told, she went through a very bleak period; but, inside of her was a steel resilience that gave her strength. I saw it in her in middle school, and I saw that same sense of determination in the checkout line. These type of traits cannot be measured on a standardized test.

This book is not a one size fits all referendum on how to fix the issues regarding education in urban schools. I don't profess to be that brilliant; and I honestly believe if someone had the answer, we would be using that method. But I am a teacher, and proud of the profession I chose. I simply wanted to shine the light on a few conversations I've had with my students who have caused me to change the way I teach. As a human being traveling in this world, it is important I never stop learning. As a Black woman educator, I understand the craft of teaching is fluid. Let me be clear: I chose this profession. No one knocked on my door and asked if I would like a job in the school down the street from my house. I voluntarily went to school, took out loans, purchased books, applied and signed a contract to pair my book knowledge with a district curriculum to increase student achievement.

Each school year brings a different set of students and new trials. What works one year may not work the next. The only constant in the room should be a thoughtful, open, forgiving, teaching and learning, empathetic adult who believes all children have the capacity to learn. This person comes in many forms both male and female. He or she comes from various races, religions and creeds, while representing all age groups from young to old.

When I began teaching, I was startled at the number of coworkers who talked negatively about the professions and the belief that they felt powerless. There was a constant hum of complaining. The refrain I heard repeatedly was "no one ever listens". This crew talked negatively about the students, the administrators, the district office, the superintendent and cabinet, the community, parents and the curriculum. I heard complaints about everything! And I was disappointed.

Instead of joining this chorus, I aligned myself with people who had spirits of excellence. I humbled myself to learn from my friends. In the Bible, Proverbs 27:17 says "As iron sharpens iron, so one person sharpens another." Because of this group, I learned that my middle school students, no matter how they looked or spoke, were not mini-adults. They were fallible kids who needed structure, guidance and a reason to learn. I learned to settle the class down, provide whole group instruction, and work with students based on what they needed, not what I wanted to teach.

My associates assisted me in changing my language and manner. My straight forward, abrupt and clipped tone had to be softened if I wanted my group to be open to my teaching. I changed my verbiage from "because I said so" to "because I asked you to". I realized when I asked students to participate in their process of learning, they were more receptive.

I created a word wall of kind phrases, like thank you, excuse me, yes or no, please and you're welcome. Words that students were not used to hearing from their teachers, and were not asked to use with each other. Politeness, I found, goes a long way. These actions are small things, but important nonetheless. The use of soft words and language provided a departure for many of my students from their home lives.

Of course, there are those students who mistake kindness for weakness. As a new teacher, I heard our in school suspension teacher say one day, "They [the student's] don't think fat meat is greasy." This is a term I have heard in Kansas City again and again. It is a way for a teacher to say I don't want to, but I can show my mean and tough side if necessary. For that small group of students who must be shown the punitive side of a teacher, I say show him or her. A teacher does not have to be loud or embarrass a student in front of the class in order for their discipline to be effective. In fact, being quiet, steady and deliberate in the delivery of chastisement is often more effective. Quiet correction conveys business, but it also provides the student with a discreet way to correct their behavior.

The first step in helping an out of control student is by contacting a parent or guardian immediately. If you have an established relationship with the home, a teacher has more leverage and assistance in working with a student to correct improper behavior. It could be something small or large, but a parent is more likely to share family issues when they know the teacher has their child's best interest at heart.

Using your schools safety team protocols for students who continuously display aggressive or inappropriate forms of behavior that endanger the student or class is another way to help disconnected students. Ask your student's friends what is going on? There is usually one or two who will quietly let you know what is happening. Make sure to let your team lead and administrators know what is taking place and document your conversations, suggestions and course of actions.

Teachers never stop trying to reach kids. Being a teacher can be a thankless job. Everyone knows how to teach; the media, big business leaders, university professors, new college graduates and anyone with a brain believe they have a formula to make students successful. I was one of those people, until I entered the profession.

Being a teacher has been my most fulfilling job. It is not the career I initially chose, but it is the profession in which I have excelled and continue to enjoy. My friends who have not talked to me in years often laugh at the notion of me being an educator. Once we start talking, the hilarity disappears, and admiration takes over. Being an educator is what I was born to do, and I don't want to stop in the classroom. I have a desire to develop a teaching methodology and open a school. An institution where I can impart the strategies my mother, my mentors and my peers instilled in me. I long to create an environment where students learn, grow, dream and become the leaders of tomorrow. I want all children and young people to obtain an education that creates the same sense of inquisitiveness and self-worth I have been allowed to develop.

In the end, as I work with students in the inner city, I pray our families brand them with hope, love, a feeling of safety, and the belief all can flourish and become constructive contributors to our society. A good education can provide social and academic skills in a tumultuous world.

We, who choose to teach, select the one profession that touches the lives of almost every person in this country. As teacher of children, it is imperative I act with integrity, and recognize how my words and deeds positively or negatively tattoo and impact our next generation of adults.

Reflection Notes

What is your story?

_____

_____

_____

_____

_____

_____

_____

_____

_____

_____

_____

_____

_____

_____

_____

_____

_____

_____

_____

Reflection Notes

Websites and Articles:

1. _____

2. _____

3. _____

4. _____

5. _____

6. _____

7. _____

Institution, District or Local Resources:

1. _____

2. _____

3. _____

4. _____

5. _____

6. _____

7. _____

Reflection Notes

Action Plan: _____

Date: _____

_____

_____

_____

_____

_____

_____

_____

_____

_____

_____

_____

_____

_____

_____

_____

_____

_____

_____

Me and My Mama's Tattoo

References

1. Payne Ph.D., Rubey K., "Teaching: Not a Discipline for the Faint of Heart." http://teaching.monster.com/benefits/articles/3524-teaching-not-a-discipline-for-the-faint-of-heart (last accessed 15 January 2013)

2. Dictionary.com—http://dictionary.reference.com/browse/tattoo?s=ts obtained 1/15/2013

3. Koebler, Jason. "National High School Graduation Rates Improve." *U.S. News & World Report*. U.S. News & World Report, 11 June 2011. Web. 10 Mar. 2013.

4. www.blackboysreport.org/national-summary/state-of-the-states obtained 3/10/13

5. Greenwood, Shannon, Andrew Perrin, and Maeve Duggan. "Social Media Update 2016." *Pew Research Center: Internet, Science & Tech*. Pew Research, 11 Nov. 2016. Web. 19 Dec. 2016.

6. Strauss, Dirk. "Power In Your Palm: The Computing Power In Today's Smartphones." *Bit Rebels*. Bit Rebels, 28 Jan. 2012. Web. 13 Apr. 2013.

7. "EMPLOYMENT." *BlackDemographics.com*. 2010 US Bureau of Labor Statistics, n.d. Web. 10 Mar. 2013.

8. US Census Bureau Public Information Office. "Census Bureau Releases 2011 American Community Survey Estimates - American Community Survey (ACS) - Newsroom - U.S. Census Bureau." *US Census Bureau Public Information Office*. US Census Bureau, 10 Mar. 2013. Web. 19 Dec. 2016.

9. US Census Bureau Public Information Office. "Facts for Features — Back to School: 2011-2012 - Facts for Features & Special Editions - Newsroom - U.S. Census Bureau." *US Census Bureau Public Information Office*. Census Bureau Public Information Office, 27 June 2011. Web. 16 Jan. 2013

10. "Missouri State Archives Guide to African American History." *Missouri Digital Heritage*. Office of Secretary of State, 2007. Web. 08 Feb. 2013.

11. Smith, Maurice, and Linda Lemasters. "What Happened to All of the Black Principals After Brown?" *International Journal of Educational Leadership Preparation* 5.4 (2010): n. pag.*OpenStax CNX.* National Counsel of Professors of Educational Administration, Oct. 2010. Web. 8 Feb. 2013.

12. Strauss, Valerie. "For First Time, Minority Students Expected to Be Majority in U.S. Public Schools This Fall." *The Washington Post.* WP Company, 21 Aug. 2014. Web. 19 Dec. 2015.

13. Rich, Motoko. "Segregation Prominent in Schools, Study Finds." *The New York Times.* The New York Times, 19 Sept. 2012. Web. 8 Feb. 2013

14. Rahulmohan11. "Descend to Ascend: To Rise, One Must Fall." *SportsKeeda.* SportsKeeda, 7 Aug. 2012. Web. 10 Mar. 2013.

15. "KEY THEORISTS." *Behaviour Management - WHAT IS CLASSROOM MANAGEMENT.* Behaviour Management, n.d. Web. 27 Aug. 2015.

16. "Definitions of Food Security." *USDA ERS - Definitions of Food Security.* US Dept of Agriculture Economic Research Service, 14 Oct. 2016. Web. 14 Jan. 2016.

17. "Key Statistics & Graphics." *USDA ERS - Key Statistics & Graphics.* US Dept of Agriculture Economic Research Service, 11 Oct. 2016. Web. 19 Dec. 2016.

18. "Benefits of School Breakfast | No Kid Hungry | The Center for Best Practices." *Benefits of School Breakfast | No Kid Hungry | The Center for Best Practices.* Share Our Strengths, 2014. Web. 19 Feb. 2016

19. Lhaman, Catherine E., and Vanita Gupta. Letter to Dear Colleague. 8 Dec. 2014. US Dept of Ed Office of Civil Rights, 8 Dec. 2014. Web. 25 Jan. 2016

20. "Key Facts: Youth in the Justice System." *Campaign for Youth Justice.* N.p., Apr. 2012. Web. 25 Jan. 2016.

21. United States. Cong. Department of Education. *Guidance Concerning State and Local Responsibilities Under the Gun-Free Schools Act.* 107 Cong. Cong. Doc. N.p.: n.p., n.d. Jan. 2004. Web. 19 Feb. 2016.

22. Gallup, Inc. "Gallup Review: Black and White Attitudes Toward Police." *Gallup.com*. Gallup, 20 Aug. 2014. Web. 9 Feb. 2016.

23. U.S. Department of Education, Office of Planning, Evaluation and Policy Development, Policy and Program Studies Service, The State of Racial Diversity in the Educator Workforce, Washington, D.C. 2016. Web. 19 Dec. 2016.

24. *Every Kid Needs a Champion*. Perf. Rita Pierson. *Www.ted.com*. TED Talks, May 2013. Web. Aug. 2013.

www.ingramcontent.com/pod-product-compliance
Lightning Source LLC
Chambersburg PA
CBHW072239290326
41934CB00008BB/1344